Praise for
Profitable Expectations: An Accountant Rises to the Challenge

"I have followed Doug and used him extensively in the past 20 years to assist me in getting a grip on the "True Economic Value" of my companies. This latest book *Profitable Expectations: An Accountant Rises to the Challenge* comes at a perfect time to transform the thinking of my newest company. The story line has made it very easy for my CFO and Controller to understand the complexities of our organization and not be intimidated from non-accountants like myself. The book has served as a reference and new set of tools to break through the paradigms in their education and experience. I have made the book required reading of my operations managers to get both groups aligned and thinking collectively. What a difference this is making."
   —Kenneth P. Oberholz, President/CEO Lincoln Manufacturing Inc.

"This book has thorough coverage of a wide range of accounting topics and is very helpful as an accounting refresher of how we as accountants need to rise to the emerging challenges. Well-written and easy to understand without technical jargon, it's a valuable compendium of accounting knowledge. Highly recommended!"
                         —Liv A. Watson, Sr. Director of Strategic
                         Customer Initiatives, Workiva, Inc.

"This book fills a need in both general business and accounting literature. For too long the 'Pygmalion principle' has been applied to accountants; decision makers' limited expectations have kept accountants from becoming value-adding resources to their organizations."
   —James Ayers CMC, Principal. CC̄   t Consultants LLC

"*Profitable Expectatio.   ι the critical role of managerial accoun   ical storytelling that makes it simple t   ...drives home a point that the role of an accoι   ...only to count the beans, but also to help grow them."
                         —Chris Domanski, Senior Manager—Direct Sourcing and
                 Optimization, Nexteer Automotive & President of the Society of
                 Product Cost Engineering and Analysis (SPCEA)

"*Profitable Expectations: An Accountant Rises to the Challenge* is a surprising read which led me on a path transforming my view of how to successfully grow a manufacturing business. As I followed the story through the kinds of discussions and meetings in my career in industry, my mental journey was similar to the one traveled by the central figure, an experienced yet open minded financial executive. This book will entertain and inform any executive seeking truth, not just tradition, enabling sound decision-making to quickly guide company financial performance to next-level profitability."
—Edward Potoczak, President and Director of Professional Services,
Oakstone Group, LLC

"On several occasions I have had the honor of experiencing Doug Hicks in one of his lectures on Managerial Costing. I have read his book *Profitable Expectations: An Accountant Rising to the Challenge* with the same enthusiasm. It is fascinating how Doug talks about the career of his protagonist Marcella. The combination of professional depth, a glimpse into the maturing of Marcella's insights, and a pinch of humor inspires the reader of the book. Almost unnoticed but captivating, the reader is immersed in the world of the controller and learns the art of cost modelling along the value chain of *PlumbCo.*

With the book *Profitable Expectations* Doug confirms my conviction that financial executives heavily influence the role an accountant plays in an organization. It is the information requested by decision makers that allows financial controllers to provide valuable input beyond traditional accounting information. This book is enlightening and a recommendation to all accountants as well as decision makers."
—Rüdiger Stern, Vice President Professional Services | President
FACTON, Inc. (North America)

"Douglas T. Hicks captures the spirit of our IMA (Institute of Management Accountants) founder, Major J. Lee Nicholson, along with our core values as an organization. The true camaraderie among IMA members and our willingness to help one another on our professional journeys are portrayed very accurately in this fun-to-read story with real value-add business applications. Among the highlights is the story of controller, Marcella DeCou, being promoted to

CEO due to her intelligence, business acumen, accounting technical knowledge, leadership capabilities, appreciation for others' contributions, and ability to truly practice diversity, equity, and inclusion. An excellent must-read with many practical management accounting insights for any manufacturing or warehousing organization. It also includes an Excel download to help readers practice the value-add model described."

—**Ginger White, CMA, CSCA, MBA, MSSF, SSBB, SSMBB &**
Global IMA Chair 2018–2019

"Number-crunching, model building, predictive analytics: who could ask for more from a story of a successful controller? In this age of automation and digital transformation, we should all ask for more, and this story delivers. It showcases the value of complementing the quantitative skills with those soft skills of open-mindedness, inquisitiveness, and collaboration that have become so highly valued. Not since The Goal have I considered using a novel like this in my classroom."

—**Paul E Juras, PhD, CMA, CPA, Vander Wolk Professor of**
Management Accounting and Operational Performance,
Babson College & Global IMA Chair 2020–2021

"In today's business environment of big data and countless transactions, identifying relevant business data is critical to decision-making. In *Profitable Expectations*, Doug Hicks provides an alternative to the checklists and templates commonly used to identify and solve the issues faced by accounting and finance in providing relevant and actionable costing information through a story—similar to the groundbreaking book, The Goal, by Eliyahu M. Goldratt—of a mid-sized company controller faced with those problems. The story highlights the benefits of mentoring, building relationships, developing staff, and focusing on the organization's goals and objectives when solving business problems. A welcome and fresh approach to management accounting for everyone, both accountants and non-accountants alike."

—**Gary Kapanowski, Contributing Editor,**
Journal of Cost Management

PROFITABLE EXPECTATIONS

AN
ACCOUNTANT
RISING TO THE
CHALLENGE

A NOVEL

DOUGLAS T. HICKS

Copyrighted Material

Profitable Expectations

Copyright © 2020 by Douglas T. Hicks. All Rights Reserved.

No part of this publication may be reproduced, stored in a retrieval system or transmitted, in any form or by any means—electronic, mechanical, photocopying, recording or otherwise—without prior written permission from the publisher, except for the inclusion of brief quotations in a review.

For information about this title or to order other books and/or electronic media, contact the publisher:
Profitability Analytics Center of Excellence (PACE)
www.profitability-analytics.org
ProfitabilityAnalytics@gmail.com

ISBN: 978-1-7356796-0-0 (print)
       978-1-7356796-1-7 (eBook)

Printed in the United States of America

Cover and Interior design: 1106 Design

To Judi, my bride of 51 years who makes "sheltering in place"
seem more like a second honeymoon,

and

my colleagues at the Profitability Analytics Center of
Excellence (PACE)
who somehow talked me into writing this story:

Raef Lawson
Kip Krumwiede
Monte Swain
Larry White &
Gary Cokins

A copy of the Excel-based cost model developed by PlumbCo and used in the course of the story in this book can be downloaded at http://www.dthicksco.com/plumbco/. Feel free to download the model and "play along" with Marcella and Jim as they use it to develop insightful information that will help enhance their company's performance.

Chapter 1

Monday mornings haven't been the same for Marcella since "The Admiral" took over as CEO three months ago. During her first three years as controller at PlumbCo, she spent the first few hours each Monday morning putting together her department's "plan of attack" for the week. This wasn't too difficult because she pretty much knew what each week would bring. Her finance staff's work was governed by weekly, monthly, quarterly, and annual cycles. Each cycle had a proven routine that got the bills paid, receivables collected, forecasts done, and results reported. Her new CEO's Monday-morning routine, however, changed all that.

"The Admiral" was Alex Johnson III, a childhood friend of PlumbCo's owner, Jake Ullrey. Jake had replaced his father as CEO 20 years ago and had built the company from a small molding shop into the $20 million organization it is today. Prior to taking over as CEO, he had worked at PlumbCo in various positions under his dad for nearly a quarter century. As he entered his early sixties, however, Jake decided it was time to slow down and enjoy the fruits of his labor. Unfortunately, his management style had been directive: He made all the key decisions based on his experience and intuition without much input from his staff.

His implicit view was that employees were there to carry out his directions, not to advise him or make decisions. As a consequence, no one within the organization had been groomed to take over when he stepped down. Enter "The Admiral."

Alex Johnson had recently returned to live in his old hometown after a successful career with the Navy, where he had attained the rank of admiral. He soon found, however, that retirement was not exactly his cup of tea. Although he enjoyed the time he could now spend at the club playing golf and tennis, he missed the challenges of leadership and expressed this feeling to his old friend Jake during a round of golf. Over lunch in the club lounge after their day on the links, Jake suggested to Alex that he take over the reins at PlumbCo, at least for a few years. That would give Jake time to find someone who could run the company for him long term. The idea appealed to Alex, and they agreed that Jake would transition to chairman of the board while Alex would take over PlumbCo's day-to-day operations as CEO.

As Marcella sat down to begin planning her week this Monday morning, a head popped through her door and asked, "Hey Marcella, have you got a few minutes?" It was Alex.

"Sure," Marcella replied, knowing full well that "a few minutes" actually meant at least a half hour. "How was your weekend?"

"Saturday wasn't so hot, I shot an 85. But I did come back with a 79 on Sunday. How was yours?"

"We packed up the kids and visited Paul's folks at the lake. I enjoy visiting the in-laws and seeing the kids have fun in the water, but weekend excursions with the family take a lot out of me."

In the three months since Alex became her boss, Marcella had become comfortable with his casual and collegial management style. It was the complete opposite of Jake's approach to management, and it gave her the confidence to pose a type of question she never would have considered asking Jake.

"How did a naval officer have time to get so good at golf anyway? I've never been able to break 90."

A wide grin grew on Alex's face.

"I got pretty good at the game when I used to caddy at the club as a kid. The club was closed on Mondays and the caddies were allowed to play all day for free. I got to be pretty chummy with old John, who was the pro back then, and he gave me a lot of tips. An officer in the Navy also has a lot more opportunities for recreational activities than you might think.

"By the way, I played Sunday with Theron Papasifakis. He's the chairman of TP Industries and a very interesting guy. He used to be in charge of acquisitions for Costa Corporation before he and a couple of his more well-to-do friends started TPI. Five years ago, they bought a $5 million stamping company and have since become a $50 million outfit by buying and restructuring small to mid-sized companies. Most of them would fall into the category of durable goods manufacturers."

"Is he one of those turnaround specialists?" asked Marcella. "Or one of those private equity investors who buys pigs, covers them with makeup, and then sells them to people he can convince that the pigs are really Miss America?"

"No," Alex said. "He doesn't look for companies that are losing money or in any kind of financial difficulty. Instead, he looks for moderately successful companies that he believes are underachieving."

"Does he restructure their financing, their operations, or what?" asked Marcella.

"It sounds like he pretty much restructures his acquisitions' overall operations," replied Alex. "He's found that many, if not most, companies have no idea of where they make money and where they lose money, which assets produce profits and which ones don't. They have products that drain away the profits being generated by other products and markets and customers whose losses offset the profits from other markets and customers."

Marcella looked a bit puzzled. "Doesn't the accounting information at these companies provide their management with that information? Haven't they been audited?"

"From what he tells me, all of these companies have had audited financial statements attested to by independent accountants. They all follow the appropriate financial accounting rules and regulations yet still don't seem to have a clue as to where the profits do or don't come from. By the way, what do you know about models?"

"Models? Models of what kind?" replied Marcella. "An underfed woman employed to display fashions? A particular style of car? A prototype? 'Model' can mean a lot of things."

"No," said Alex, "I mean models as a general concept. Something we create to understand more complicated things. Like the economy ... or how to raise children ... or what kind of diet will help us stay healthy ... or what an atom looks like. Theron talks a lot about the importance of models, especially when it comes to decision-making."

Marcella thought for a few moments. "I have given a lot of thought to all those topics, except maybe what an atom looks like, but I can't say I've ever included the concept of model in those thoughts. Those all just seem like something someone teaches you or something that's intuitive. Why do you ask?"

"Well, Theron believes that accountants lack an understanding of models and that lack of understanding is a major reason why the information they give decision-makers is generally useless and sometimes totally misleading."

"That's a pretty strong criticism of accountants. Do you think the information we provide here is 'generally useless and sometimes totally misleading'?"

"It's not something that even occurred to me until this weekend. Theron has proven to be a pretty smart guy, and I put a lot of stock into things he says. It seems to me that you and your crew are very good at what you do, but I am beginning to wonder if there's something systemic, something embedded in the fundamental way accountants do things, that impacts the numbers they provide to decision-makers."

The purpose of this Monday's chat with the boss was becoming clear. Marcella realized that she was about to be given some kind of assignment. So much for her plans for the week.

Alex looked at his watch. "I've got to run. A group of our sales reps are visiting the office this morning. Give some thought to the connection between models and accounting between now and next Monday, and we'll pick up this conversation again then."

Great, thought Marcella, *finish closing the books, do the monthly reports, make sure we've got enough cash to pay the bills, and get into the philosophy of models in accounting.* With that, she got to work doing what controllers do to earn their keep.

Chapter 2

By Thursday, Marcella had managed to squeeze in a little internet research on models, but she wasn't very confident she had gained much insight into whatever it was that Alex was after. When 4:30 rolled around, she packed up for the day and headed out to the monthly dinner meeting held by her chapter of the Institute of Management Accountants. Although she was looking forward to hearing from this month's speaker, who was giving an update on changes in the health care regulations, she also hoped that some of her fellow IMA members could give her some insights on models and accounting.

At about a quarter past five, she arrived at the Kingsley Arms, the same hotel where the IMA chapter had been holding its meetings for a couple of decades, and she saw her college classmate, Caroline Perry, walking to the hotel from her spot in the parking lot.

"Caroline!" she shouted. Caroline stopped, saw it was Marcella and waited until she could catch up. "How've you been? Haven't seen you the past few months."

"We've been pretty busy at the shop," she smiled and then added, "although that's a pretty weak excuse for not being at a meeting since Christmas. I really just didn't see speakers on topics in which I was interested, and I figured it wasn't worth coming just for the networking. But you know what? I found I actually missed the monthly night out and catching up with the chapter regulars. I must have learned my lesson since I'm not really interested in an update on health care regulations but I'm here anyway."

The two caught up on news of their families and friends while they signed in and picked up refreshments from the bar.

"Tell me, Caroline," Marcella said as she took her first sip, "have you ever had any kind of discussion about models in accounting with a professor, a colleague, or anyone else?"

"No, I can't say that I have."

"Have you ever read anything about the topic?"

"No. Is it something I should know about?"

"Probably not," Marcella admitted, "but my boss seems to think it's something I ought to know more about, and I'm not even sure what it is he's talking about. I'm hoping someone here tonight can help me out. Any little hint or bit of information might help." With that, they both slipped into the cluster of people doing some pre-presentation socializing.

Marcella felt a close enough connection with about half of those attending the meeting to approach them, either before the speaker's rather dry discussion of health care administration or during the post-presentation dinner, and she asked if they had any insight regarding the connection between models and accounting. It didn't help. About half of them just looked at her blankly, and none of them could provide any useful information. Quite disappointed, she began packing up to head home.

As she said her goodnights to her friends, a one-armed, elderly man whom she did not know personally, but had often noticed at these meetings, approached her and said, "Excuse me, Mrs. DeCou. Did I understand that you were interested in the connection between models and accounting?"

Not much was known about this quiet old gentleman. The chapter members referred to him as "the Major," but no one was quite sure why. He'd been attending monthly meetings as long as anyone could remember, but he wasn't active in any other chapter activities. He just arrived at each meeting, found a fairly isolated place to sit, sipped what appeared to be a Manhattan, listened to the speaker's presentation, and then quietly left. He didn't avoid the other chapter members, but he didn't actively pursue conversations with them either, and he never revealed much about himself.

"Why, yes," Marcella responded to his inquiry, "I am trying to learn something about the connection between the models and practice of accounting."

"Perhaps I can help," the Major smiled. "Do you have a few moments now? I might be able to shed a little light on the topic. We can find a spot to talk in the lobby or, if you'd rather, at a table in the Kingsley Arms' lounge."

Marcella hesitated. Meeting a relative stranger after an IMA meeting was not something she would normally do, but he seemed genuine, and there was still time before her family expected her at home. So she said "Sure," and the two retired to a table in the hotel's sparsely populated lounge.

After the waitress had brought her a glass of wine and him another Manhattan the Major asked her, "Tell me, how did this rather offbeat topic become important to you?"

Marcella related the conversation she had had with Alex that Monday.

"I see," said the Major thoughtfully. "Tell me, how much do you know about nutrition? Would you consider yourself an expert in the subject?"

"No," replied Marcella. "I know a little about it, but I'm no expert."

"I overheard you talking to your friend about your husband and children, so I'm guessing you plan meals for your family, right?"

"That I do."

"You do want your family's meals to help promote good health for all of your family members, don't you?"

"Of course."

"In that case, how do you make sure you're not feeding them the kind of diet that promotes obesity, high blood pressure, diabetes, or any other health issue you'd really like to avoid?"

Marcella was beginning to wonder where this guy was going with these questions.

"I believe I know enough to keep us on the right track," she answered. "I make sure we all eat enough fruits and vegetables. We only have red meat a couple of times a week, and when we do, I make sure it's pretty lean. I make sure the kids have a good breakfast and I limit their sweets. I read the labels on stuff I buy to make sure it's not too high in sugar, sodium, or the bad fats."

"That sounds good, but how do you know those are the right things to do when you're not an expert on nutrition?"

Marcella was really beginning to wonder what this had to do with models, but she still had half a glass of wine left, so she figured she'd play along for a while longer.

"I believe they're all based on pretty accurate assessments made by those who are experts," she replied. "I've got a lot of confidence in the fact that they're all good representations of what it takes to have a healthy diet."

"But they're not comprehensive, are they? They don't represent the entirety of what it takes to optimize each of your individual family member's health."

"No, but I think they're good enough to guide me in putting together some pretty healthy menus."

"Do you know why you believe that?"

"Why I believe that, huh? I can't say that I could describe why."

"The field of nutrition is wide and complex with a lot of variables that can impact what's good for one person versus what's good for another. It's far too complicated for anyone, even a nutritionist, to understand fully. Yet you, a controller, wife, and mother, still have to make important dietary decisions within such a complex environment. In order to do so, you've determined what you believe to be the key elements surrounding nutrition and how those elements relate to each other. You use them as a substitute for a more complex reality that you cannot fully comprehend.

"What you've done," continued the Major, "is create a model of reality. It's not actually reality, but an understandable construct that enables you to deal with something that's not fully understandable. You use that model to guide your decision-making."

"I guess that's true," interjected Marcella. "You might say I've dumbed it down so I can use what I know to make decisions that I am confident are best for my family."

"I wouldn't call it dumbing down," replied the Major, "I would call it being smart. Understanding that you don't know—actually, you can't know—everything about a phenomenon that has a critical impact on you, but being astute enough to create a reasonably valid model of that phenomenon that enables you to make informed decisions, is a sign of intelligence.

"But tell me," he added, "what if this model you've developed turns out to be wrong? What if it doesn't actually provide you with a valid picture of reality? You'd believe it to be true, but it wouldn't be. It would not represent reality."

"Then I'd be making pretty bad decisions, wouldn't I?" answered Marcella. "I'd be feeding my family meals that would have a detrimental impact on their health."

"That's right," replied the Major, "you'd believe you're doing the right thing, yet you'd be doing the wrong thing." A grin grew on the Major's face. "I bet you're wondering what this has to do with accounting."

"That question had occurred to me."

"Tell me, how would you describe your company's business?"

"PlumbCo is a manufacturer of plumbing products."

"You manufacture plumbing products to the customer's order and ship them directly to your customers' locations?"

"No, we don't manufacture to customer order or ship them immediately after production. We manufacture based on a forecast of customer demand, hold them in our warehouse, and then ship when a customer order arrives."

"Is your warehouse pretty large? Are there a lot of people working in it?"

"Oh yes, it occupies about one-third of our overall floor space and has about two dozen workers assigned to it."

"Do you have a cost accounting system?"

"Of course. We have an excellent standard costing system that is part of the company's overall ERP system. We've got standards for every part we make. Our inventories are very accurate. We seldom have a significant book-to-physical adjustment after taking our physical inventories. And the auditors are always happy with our inventory accounting. I guess that should be expected; they helped us design and implement the system we use."

"Do you have a separate way of accounting for the warehouse?"

"A separate way? Sure. It has its own budget, and we treat it as a separate cost center in the accounting records."

"Is its cost assigned to your products or customers?"

"Some of the warehouse cost is included in overhead and that gets assigned to our products as part of the overhead rate."

"And the rest of the warehouse cost?"

"It just becomes part of our general and administrative expense."

"Does that make sense to you? Does it reflect a good model of your business?"

"I guess so. It complies with generally accepted accounting principles; the auditors see to that. As far I know, it's the usual way manufacturers like us handle their accounting. Assign all the legitimate inventoriable costs to your products, and the rest is just a cost of running the business. Don't you think it make sense?"

"Your company is a complex structure with a wide variety of activities taking place every day. Having a complete understanding of all its intricacies and interrelationships may be possible, but not very practical. However, a sound understanding of what its various activities are, how they interrelate with each other, and how they relate to your products and customers is essential if you're to make informed business decisions. In accounting, you monetize those activities and relationships so decision-makers can understand, in advance, the likely financial impact of the decisions they must make. Just as your ability to make good dietary decisions for your family are a function of the accuracy and validity of your model of nutrition, your company's decision-makers' ability to make good business decisions is a function of the accuracy and validity of the model accounting creates to process financial information. If that model is not a valid representation of the company's operations, decisions will be based on erroneous or incomplete cost information.

"I would suggest to you that your accounting model of PlumbCo is invalid and does not accurately reflect the fundamental economics that underlie the business. Although it may be good enough to accurately reflect the financial results of the entire company after the fact, it does not provide decision-makers with the quality financial information they need to make sound business decisions."

Marcella was taken aback the Major's very direct and blunt assessment based on the little information she provided to him.

"What's wrong with it?" she protested.

"It's getting pretty late," he answered, "and getting past my bedtime. Let me leave you with this: PlumbCo is not a manufacturer; it is actually two companies. One is a manufacturer that has only one customer—the warehouse. The other is the warehouse itself, a distributor that has many customers, but only one supplier—the manufacturing facility. It's two totally different businesses, and the same accounting model doesn't fit both of them.

"I'll undoubtedly be here again next month. If you'd like to give our conversation some thought, I'd be happy to meet with you again afterwards and continue our discussion."

Still somewhat peeved by the way the conversation ended, Marcella said she thought she'd be at the next meeting and would probably be able to meet afterwards. She wasn't too certain she wanted to meet with this know-it-all again, but she wasn't too certain she didn't. With that, they finished their drinks, wished each other a pleasant evening, and headed to the parking lot.

Chapter 3

On Monday, Alex stopped by for his weekly chat and plopped himself down in the visitor's chair facing his controller. After describing his not-so-successful weekend on the links and discussing her family's weekend high jinks, he asked if she'd given any thought to last week's topic.

"As a matter of fact, I have," she replied. "I even had a chat about it with a somewhat mysterious old guy who attends our monthly IMA meetings."

"A mysterious old guy?" Alex responded. "What do you mean, 'mysterious old guy'?"

"Oh, he's only mysterious in that none of us know much about him and he doesn't say much. The members refer to him as 'the Major,' and he comes to almost every meeting but just sits in the back and listens. He's real old school as well. He's always dressed impeccably—he even wears three-piece suits! Who dresses that way nowadays? And he has only one arm."

A grin grew on Alex's face. "I like three-piece suits. I kinda miss the days when everyone wore suits and dressed sharp to work and work functions. I acquiesced to casual dress here at PlumbCo only because that's what people here wanted, and it wasn't worth making a big deal over. As long as people get their work done, I don't care what they wear, within reason, of course."

Oops! thought Marcella. *I blew that one.*

"Anyway, why do they call him 'the Major'?" asked Alex.

"I have no idea. Someone may have heard he was once in the military. Maybe that's how he lost his arm."

"It couldn't have been the Navy. We don't have majors in the Navy, we have lieutenant commanders. Anyway, if he just sits in the back and listens, how did you happen to have a chat with him?"

"I had been asking some of the folks at the meeting about the connection between models and accounting—to no avail, I might add—and he must have overheard me because as I was getting ready to leave, he approached me and asked if I'd like to talk about the subject. I didn't want to offend him. Although a bit unusual, he seemed to be a nice old gentleman, so I agreed."

Marcella went on to relate her conversation with the Major.

"What do you think of his assessment?" asked Alex.

"I admit I was offended at the time. He was so blunt and quick with his comments after I really hadn't given him all that much background information. But after mulling over his remarks this weekend, I got the feeling there might be something to them."

"How's that?"

"Our accounting system does assume we manufacture products and sell them to customers. But you could also view us the way he did. We manufacture products and sell them to an in-house distributor. That in-house distributor then holds them and fills orders as they come along. Even though we're all under one roof, we could be viewed as two separate businesses.

If that's really the case, the model on which we base our account-ing practices could be wrong."

Alex was interested. "How would the accounting system be different if it did follow the Major's model?"

"I don't really know," admitted Marcella. "Every manufac-turer I've dealt with over the years, including those I worked with in public accounting, did their accounting the same way we do. It follows generally accepted accounting principles, passes audits, and seems to make everyone happy. Yet, I can't find a hole in the old guy's logic."

"Maybe this is something we should look into. Why don't you do a little research into this? Spend some time with Rich Vivian out in the warehouse and see if you can come up with some ideas."

The two of them then went on to discuss the previous month's results and the information Alex would need for the upcoming board meeting.

Chapter 4

Richard Vivian had been managing PlumbCo's warehouse operation for about five years. He began working for the company during summers while he was still in high school, and he signed on full time as soon as he graduated. He had done just about every job in the warehouse before being named its manager, and he was proud of his intimate knowledge of every warehouse function. He did feel, however, that his team of warehouse workers were looked upon as second-class citizens by the company's management—not nearly as important as the manufacturing team. This feeling could sometimes be detected in his working relationships with other managers. Marcella was aware of this, so she approached him with caution.

"Hey Rich," she said as she approached him after a staff meeting, "got a minute?"

"Just a minute?" he replied.

"Okay. Five minutes then."

"Sure, I've got five minutes. Always have time for the person who controls the purse strings. But just five minutes. I've got a lot on my plate today."

"Five minutes will do. I just want to see if you can set aside a couple of hours sometime during the next week or so that we can spend talking about the warehouse."

"Talking about the warehouse?"

"Yeah, talking about the warehouse."

"What for?"

Marcella could see a bit of a defensive posture developing. "I've been working here for about four years now, and I haven't really learned much about what goes on out there. Most of the time we focus on the manufacturing side and take the important work you people do for granted." She thought a dose of flattery might soften his attitude. "I'd really like to understand warehouse operations a lot more."

"Oh," replied Rich, "if that's the case, I might be able to set aside a couple of hours early next week. Keep in mind that our session might get interrupted. Emergencies do keep cropping up. Tuesday mornings are probably the best time. Mid-morning maybe?"

"How about we pencil in 10:00 Tuesday morning? Let me know if something interferes, but if I don't hear anything from you I'll be at your office at 10 on Tuesday."

"Sounds like a plan," replied Rich. And with that, they headed back to their offices.

Marcella heard nothing from Rich, so she arrived at his office on Tuesday morning at 10:00 sharp. He wasn't there so she sat down in one of his visitors' chairs and waited. He arrived ten minutes late.

"Sorry I'm late. One of my pickers called in sick and I had to figure out how to cover for him out in the plant."

"No problem." Marcella smiled. "What's a picker?"

"I guess you don't know much about how a warehouse operates, do you?"

"That's why I'm here."

They both laughed.

"A picker is the person who gets a 'pick sheet' and then goes from place to place in the warehouse, picks the items from inventory, takes them to the shipping area, and sorts them by order."

"Is this person picking one order at a time?"

"No. The ERP system combines orders in a way that will minimize the time the picker must travel from location to location while keeping in mind the quantity of goods a picker can be reasonably expected to collect during one trip. That's the 'pick list' I mentioned. It may have several orders combined or be only one part of a large order. That's why the picker must sort them by order when he or she arrives in shipping."

"It sounds more sophisticated than I thought," said Marcella. A little more flattery wouldn't hurt in softening up Rich.

"The whole operation is pretty sophisticated. A lot more sophisticated than when I started here. We had to figure out all this stuff on our own ... with our eyeballs. We'd get the day's orders, divide them up among the pickers, and they'd figure out the best way to pick their orders. Efficiency wasn't a big issue. We figured we were successful if we got all the orders out by the end of the day."

"How's the warehouse organized?" asked Marcella. "How do you determine what goes where?"

"We have a racking system. You can visualize it as five-by-five-by-five cubes that are stacked four cubes high, with row after row of the four-cube-high towers. Each part number is assigned one or more of those cubes."

"Are they in part number order?"

"No. That would be too inefficient for picking. We've got the parts divided into three groups. An 'A' group, which includes the most popular part numbers. They're the locations we must visit the most often and hold the part numbers that turn the quickest, so they're located nearest the shipping area. The more popular of those part numbers are stored in the lower cubes so they're easier to get at.

"Then there's the 'B' group. Those part numbers are moderate in popularity and their locations visited often, but not nearly as frequently as those in the 'A' group. Finally, there's the 'C' group. Our last controller—before you—used to call that our FISH inventory."

"FISH inventory?" responded Marcella.

"Yeah, FISH inventory. It stands for First In, Still Here. It's the stuff we seldom sell but maintain in our product line to keep it complete. Some of it we pick only once or twice a month. There are even a few part numbers we touch only once or twice a year. It's located the farthest from the shipping area."

Marcella was getting interested. Warehousing involved a lot more than she thought. "So you get the product from manufacturing and put it into its assigned cube. How does it arrive from manufacturing?"

"As I'm sure you know, each part is packaged in its own retail package. A number of those packages are put in boxes depending on the 'box quantity' established by marketing, and those boxes are put on a pallet. The product is then moved to the warehouse on the pallet."

"What's a 'box quantity'?"

"That's the number of parts marketing determines is the most effective for those customers not buying onesies and twosies. We'll sell any quantity of parts, even though the onesies and twosies are a pain in the … well, you know where. We like selling full boxes whenever possible."

"So you have to break into those boxes for the onesie-twosies?"

"Yeah. There's usually one open box in the cube at any point in time for those."

"Do you store them on the pallets?"

"No. We remove them from the pallets, store the boxes in the cubes, and send the pallets back over to manufacturing."

"So storing the parts takes a bit of time?"

"You could say that. Once we take them to their cube, someone must remove the boxes from the pallets and tuck them away."

Marcella was starting to enjoy this conversation. "The four-high cubes go higher than a person can reach. How do your people reach the higher cubes?"

"We've got these rolling ladder platforms that they push around manually. A couple of years back, I tried to get management to invest in some electric stock pickers, you know, those units that can lift the picker up to pick the item and then drive them to the next location, but it got shot down. They said they needed to use their capital money to improve manufacturing."

"What happens when the product gets to shipping?"

"It depends. If there are loose packages they need to get boxed in shipping. If the order is small, we box it up and send it UPS. We have a UPS pickup every day at about 5:00. Larger orders get palletized, shrink-wrapped, and loaded on our common carrier's trailer. Each day the carrier picks up the loaded trailer and drops off an empty one."

Rich was looking at his watch. "Any other questions?" He was obviously antsy to get on with his day.

"No, not now," replied Marcella. "I think I've overdosed on warehousing already. I'll need some time to process all this information. Once I do, I'll probably have some more questions, but I really appreciate the time you've spent with me this morning."

"No problem," laughed Rich. "After all, I've got to stay on the good side of the person who controls the purse strings." He probably didn't realize he had used that expression before.

Chapter 5

Over the next few weeks, Marcella mulled over all that she had learned about the warehouse operation. Although she felt she knew a great deal more about that part of the business, she couldn't quite figure out how that impacted accounting and the idea of the accounting model. The date for her next IMA meeting rolled around, and she determined that she would seek out the Major for another chat after the meeting.

Upon arriving at the Kingsley Arms, Marcella immediately started looking for the Major but didn't see him anywhere. As she mixed with the other members, she kept one eye out for her target, but to no avail. The speaker gave his presentation on the state of the local economy and the dinner was served, but the Major was still nowhere to be found. She was quite disheartened as the meeting wound down, attendees began to leave, and it looked as if her primary reason for attending the meeting would be unfulfilled. As she began packing up to leave, however, she heard a man's voice say, "Mrs. DeCou."

She turned and saw the impeccably dressed, one-armed older gentleman. He seemed to have appeared out of nowhere.

The man smiled and said, "I took the liberty of ordering you a glass of wine, and it's waiting for you in the lounge. Would you care to join me?"

Surprised—and pleased—by his sudden appearance, she replied, "Major! Of course I would!" and the two of them headed to Kingsley Inn's lounge where a Chardonnay was awaiting her.

"I didn't see you all evening, and I thought you hadn't come to the meeting," she said.

He smiled, "I was here. I just try to stay inconspicuous. I'm an old over-the-hill accountant and try not to interfere with you young folks who are now running the world."

"Maybe you're old," she replied, "but I wouldn't say you're over the hill. After thinking about the chat we had last month, I'd say you're still on the top of your game." After the words came out, she wasn't too sure she should have started with the "maybe you're old" comment, but the big grin on his face showed that no offense had been taken.

"So," he started, "you've given my comments some thought?"

"Oh yeah, I've given them a lot of thought. I can see a lot of logic in what you said, but I'm still at a loss about what it all means and what to do." She then went on to summarize her new understanding of how PlumbCo's warehouse operates. "As you can see," she said while wrapping up her summary, "there are a lot of different activities taking place in the warehouse, but they almost all take place after the product is produced. None of them add value to the product, and, as far as I can tell, none of the costs are inventoriable. Even if they were inventoriable, I can't think of any logical way to assign them to each product."

"Why do you seem so hung up on the fact that the costs of running the warehouse aren't inventoriable?" asked the Major.

"Well, if the costs aren't inventoriable, I'm not allowed to include them as part of the cost of the product, according to generally accepted accounting principles."

"Why would you want to assign them to products?"

"Isn't the purpose of my cost accounting system to measure product cost so I can close the books and measure performance?" Marcella was getting a little flustered, but she somehow trusted the Major was leading up to something, as he was with the previous month's quiz on nutrition.

"The primary purpose of your cost accounting system is to value your inventory and measure your cost of goods sold, and it must comply with GAAP if you want to pass an audit; but is it also the purpose of your cost accounting system to provide PlumbCo's decision-makers with the cost information they need to make decisions?"

"Of course, where else would cost information come from?"

"Have you ever heard of John Maurice Clark?"

"Can't say I have."

"John Maurice Clark was an early- to mid-twentieth-century economist. Way back in 1923, he wrote a book titled *Studies in the Economics of Overhead Costs*, which introduced many of the costing concepts that are bandied about today—such as fixed and variable costs, joint costs, sunk costs, and differential costs. He also stressed the importance of including time as a factor in defining fixed and variable costs. But the most important point he emphasized was that there are different kinds of problems for which we need information about costs and that the particular information we need differs from one problem to another. One measure of cost does not fit all circumstances.

"One of the problems for which you need information about costs is the valuation of your company's inventory and measurement of its cost of goods sold. You've created a cost accounting system that complies with GAAP to solve that problem. I would suggest, however, that it is useless for anything else."

"Useless?"

"Actually, I'm trying to be polite. Dysfunctional is probably a better term."

"Dysfunctional?"

"Yes, dysfunctional. It not only generates cost information that is of no use in supporting decisions, but the information it generates often leads to decisions that are actually based on *misinformation*. Sometimes because the information is simply incorrect and other times because it's incomplete.

"Do you recall the old Stephen Stills song from the 1970s, 'Love the One You're With'? In its refrain, it has the lyrics, 'If you can't be with the one you love, honey, love the one you're with'? That's what most companies do with cost information. They don't have the cost information that they need—sometimes they don't even know what cost information they need—so they 'love the one they're with,' which is the cost information that they do have, the stuff from their cost accounting system. A system, by the way, that was not designed to provide that information."

"That song is a bit before my time, but I believe I've heard it once or twice." Marcella was getting a little irritated by the Major's way of asking her questions instead of giving her answers. *This old guy must think he's Socrates,* she thought to herself. "Can you give me an example of how the cost accounting system would fail to provide good information for decision-makers?"

"I could probably come up with dozens, but let's start with this: How would you measure customer profitability?"

"Oh, we do that all the time. Within the cost system, we sum up the total sales and cost of goods sold to the customer. The sales less the cost of sales gives us the customer's profitability. And all that information is from our cost accounting system."

"And you believe that gives you an accurate measure of the customer's profitability?"

"I do."

"Then let me ask you this. If you had two customers who bought the same 6,240 units of product at the same price annually, would their profitability be equal?"

"Sure. Their sales and cost of goods sold would both be the same."

"What if one customer gave you one order per week and you picked, packed, and shipped that customer 120 units each Friday. Meanwhile, the other customer gave you one order per month and you picked, packed, and shipped that company 520 units at the end of each month? Would their profitability still be the same?"

Marcella hesitated for a moment. She was beginning to see a point being made, but she wasn't sure yet what it was. "I'm not sure," she replied.

"Think about it. Take one part number that represents 10% of both customers' sales. Each week a picker has to go to that part number's spot in the warehouse and pick 12 items for one of the customers. The picker has to do that 52 times a year to support those sales. On the other hand, a picker has to make that trip only 12 times a year to support the same part number's sales to the other customer. Don't you think fulfillment of that part number's sales to the weekly customer would cost a lot more than the fulfillment of the monthly customer's sales of the same item? Wouldn't that make the profitability of the monthly customer greater than that of the weekly customer?"

"I see what you're getting at, but how would I incorporate that information into the cost accounting system? I can't put all those post-manufacturing costs you call 'fulfillment' into an overhead rate and include them in inventory. That's not GAAP. And how would I do it anyway? If I added it to our overhead rate, it would make each part's cost higher, but they'd still be the same."

The Major looked at his watch. "You know, it's almost 9:30. We should probably be getting along."

"But I think I'm just beginning to understand what you're talking about," Marcella protested.

"Your family is probably wondering why you're not home yet, and it's getting late for a guy my age. Let me give you a few things to think about, and we can pick up this conversation again next month.

"First, you don't have to bookkeep all the cost information you use to support your managers' decisions. Don't let debits and credits hang you up.

"Second, the purpose of the information you supply to your decisions-makers is insight. It is not the numbers themselves.

"And third, the only rule for cost information used to support decisions is that it be accurate and relevant. There is no costing equivalent of GAAP. The key is that cost information for decision-making needs to represent economic reality. You need to invent a technique for linking these warehousing costs to *customers*, not to products."

"Invent a technique?"

"Sure, be like Isaac Newton."

"Like Isaac Newton? What should I do, wait for an apple to fall on my head?"

"Sort of," laughed the Major. "That apocryphal story allegedly took place while Newton was a young man spending time in the country outside of London while Cambridge was closed down due to the plague. One of the things that occupied his time was a quest to find an explanation for the movement of the planets. Unfortunately, he found that the known mathematical processes at the time were inadequate for his purposes. So instead of giving up, he invented a process that would work. We now call it calculus. If you can't find an existing process that works, create one that does."

Before she could protest, the Major was already halfway out the door. She would have to wait until next month for any further discussion.

Chapter 6

"Wasn't last week your monthly IMA meeting?' asked Alex as he settled into a guest chair in Marcella's office the following Monday morning.

"Yeah," she replied. "Are you starting to keep track of my schedule?"

"No, but this Major guy you talked about last month has me intrigued. I figured it was about a month since you last mentioned him, so I just made a guess. Did you see him again?"

"I'm afraid so."

"You're afraid so? What does that mean?"

Marcella smiled and said, "After I talk to him, I feel that I learned something important, but I also feel more confused at the same time. He asks a lot of questions that eventually highlight problems and shoot down my current way of thinking, but then he ends the conversation without describing a solution. This time he ended our conversation by telling the story of Isaac Newton inventing calculus."

"I've got to hear about this," replied Alex while edging forward in his seat. "Tell me more."

"As you probably know, I spent several hours with Rich Vivian last month learning some of the finer points about warehousing operations. I told the Major what I had learned, and he indicated that he not only thought our cost information methodology was totally useless for anything except external financial reporting, he called it dysfunctional."

Alex began laughing. "The Major certainly doesn't pull any punches, does he?"

"He definitely says what he thinks. When I asked him to explain why he believed it was so dysfunctional, he came up with a pretty convincing example of how our method misstates customer profitability." She then went on to relate the Major's example to Alex, after which she added, "I couldn't find any flaw in his reasoning, can you?"

"No, not really. Did he give you any hint as to how we could measure customer profitability more accurately?"

"No. All he did was tell me not to worry about book-keeping everything, that the exactness of the numbers is not important, it's the insight they provide, and that the only rule for cost information used by decision-makers is that it should reflect economic reality. He said I should invent a method of connecting warehousing costs to customers. When I protested, he told the story of Newton and calculus."

"I like this guy, even if he's not a Navy man," said Alex. "I think he sees something in you that you don't yet know you have. Either that or he's trying to see if you do have that 'something.' What are you going to do now?"

"I've got to get the month closed up and the report out," replied Marcella.

"No, I mean about creating a model that links warehouse operations to customer profitability."

"A model?"

"Yeah. A model. Remember what Theron Papasifakis said about accountants and models? That the cost information accountants provide decision-makers is generally useless and sometimes misleading because they lack an understanding of models. Well, it sounds like your friend the Major is of the same mindset. His suggestion is that the model we use as a basis for measuring costs doesn't reflect the company's economic realities. The only detail assignment of costs we make is to products, but we also incur costs that are not caused by products but by our customers' behavior. We need to develop and follow a model that assigns the cost of fulfilling a customer's order to that customer. Otherwise, we won't have a good handle on customer profitability. Why don't you spend some time with Rich again and see if the two of you can come up with something?"

Great, thought Marcella, *like I don't have enough to do.* But then she caught herself. Maybe this was her chance to prove that her crew in finance wasn't just overhead, an opinion she had heard on many occasions since taking over the controllership at PlumbCo. Maybe she could come up with a different vision of the company and a new set of profit analytics that would lead PlumbCo into a more profitable future. She wasn't being presented with a problem to solve; she was being given an opportunity to show how finance can be a full partner in managing the business.

"That I'll do!" she responded and then added, "But I'd like you to do me a favor."

"You name it," replied Alex.

"I'd like you to lay a little groundwork with Rich. He's a good guy, but he does have this complex about warehousing being undervalued by the company. We had a good session last

month, but I'm afraid he might take my quizzing him again—
this time about ways to measure what's done in his arena—the
wrong way. I'm afraid he won't take this newfound attention on
the work they do to fulfill orders as a positive. He may attach
some ulterior motive that's not there."

"I understand. I've also noticed a little of that 'complex,' as
you call it, in Rich since I've been here. Consider it done."

Soon afterward, Alex had a chat with Rich about the company's desire to better understand how fulfillment efforts were
related to specific customers and suggested that he contact
Marcella to see if she had some time to discuss the topic. Within
a few hours, a meeting had been set up for the following week.

Chapter 7

Rich arrived at Marcella's office at the appointed hour—not late this time. Apparently, Alex's visit was the first time "the boss" had ever told him that his input was going to be a valuable contribution to an important initiative the company was considering. He was accustomed to receiving orders from the CEO, not being asked for his advice or opinion, and he was anxious to prove that he had a lot to contribute.

"Hey, Marcella," he said as he walked through the door, "are you ready to rock 'n roll?"

"I don't know about rocking and rolling," she replied, "but I am ready to get started on coming up with a way to address our challenge."

"And what exactly is that challenge?"

"As Alex may have told you, we've come to believe that we cannot fully understand how valuable and profitable each customer is to PlumbCo unless we can somehow attach the cost of our warehousing and fulfillment activities to customers in a way that reflects their demand for those activities." She proceeded to relate the example the Major had used to convince her of their costing model's shortcoming. "In simple terms, our challenge is to figure out a way to determine how much more profitable the customer with monthly shipments is than the one with weekly shipments."

"Where do we start?"

"This is new to me, so I'm not sure. I thought we might walk through the work done by your troops, step by step, and think about how each step relates to the customer."

"Sounds like a reasonable approach. Let's do it."

Looking at her notes from their previous meeting, Marcella said, "Well, the first thing you do is to receive the product from manufacturing and tuck it away in its assigned cube."

"That's right," responded Rich, "each product arrives in boxes on pallets. We remove the boxes from the pallets, store the boxes, and then return the pallets to manufacturing."

"And then they just sit there until somebody orders something?"

"That's about it," Rich said but then added, "other than the fact that we have to do cycle counts periodically and take a physical inventory once a year." He laughed, "Some of those babies end up being counted two or three years in a row. Still got tags on 'em from each inventory. Other than that, there's really nothing else done until an order comes."

Marcella thought for a minute and then said, "So you could say that once the product is put away in its cube, it must rent that space from the warehouse until someone buys it. Some products just rent space in the cube for a few days, while others must rent it for years. But since storage takes place before a customer order is received, it would seem to indicate that any storage cost would be related to the product, not to the customer. Does that make sense to you?"

"Yeah," replied Rich, without a lot of confidence. He was still trying to get a handle on what it was that he and Marcella were trying to accomplish. After a pause, he added, "But couldn't you also look at it this way? We tuck the product away in inventory for the customer and hold it until they ask for it. We're doing them a service by holding onto their product until they want it. Wouldn't that make it a customer-related cost, not a product-related cost?"

"I guess you could look at it that way as well." Marcella was silent for a moment. *This isn't going to be as straightforward as I had hoped,* she thought to herself. *There may be more than one right answer to any given question.* At that point, she remembered the Major's comment regarding "different costs for different purposes." *Maybe that doesn't apply only to the numbers,* she thought, *but also to the way they are put together.*

"Let's leave that up in the air for now and move on to the next step. A customer order arrives. Is that it?"

"That's what comes next," replied Rich. "Our customer service people receive an order and then enter it into the system."

"Is the work involved in entering it into the system the same for all orders?"

"Definitely not. Some customers enter orders electronically using our customer portal. That doesn't require much work at all. Others mail or fax us old-fashioned paper purchase orders. Those have to be entered into the system by the customer service folks. Still others phone in their orders. Customer service must take the phone call and enter the order while hanging on the line with the customer." Rich thought for a few moments. "That probably handles 99% of the orders."

"Is that all customer service does before an order hits the system?"

"Well, they do have to communicate by phone with the folks sending non-electronic orders when one of the items they ordered is out of stock or there's some other issue with their order. Information about out-of-stock items is sent automatically by the system to those sending electronic orders. Customer service reps seldom need to call those customers."

"Okay. The order is entered; then what happens?"

"Once the order is entered, the system does its thing. It converts the incoming orders into pick lists for the pickers. As I told you last time, that includes sorting a day's orders into pick lists that represent the most efficient way for the pickers to pick the products. A particular order's product might be split up among several pick lists, each including products from different orders. The pickers then sort the products by order when they deliver them to shipping."

Marcella was keeping careful notes of Rich's comments. There was a lot to remember, and she knew she would need to cover all the important elements of the process if she was to "invent" a model that covered them effectively.

"Let's move on to shipping," she said with a sigh. She was starting to overdose on warehousing information again.

"By the time shipping gets involved, the products have been sorted by order. Some are the loose items I mentioned last time, and some are in boxes. The system generates packing lists that tell shipping how to sort the loose items and pack them into boxes. The system also generates all of the labels and shipping documents that will be needed. The larger orders are palletized, shrink-wrapped, and loaded onto the trailer. The boxes with smaller orders are labeled and put in the holding area for the daily UPS pickup."

"That's it?" asked Marcella with a hopeful look.

"That's about it," replied Rich, "unless ..."

"Unless? Unless what?"

"Unless you want to know about returns and restocks."

"Okay, I'm game. Tell me about returns and restocks."

"Well, sometimes the customer claims we screwed up a shipment and returns some of the products. Other times, the customer is just being a jerk and sends back items they found that they really didn't need. We seldom take exception in either case and process their returns for a credit. The returns are received by receiving and sent back here to shipping. Shipping determines whether or not the returned items are still salable. If they are, they'll be entered back into the inventory system, and pickers will return them to their cube for sale later on. Customer service will process the paperwork."

"What about the unsalable items?"

"Most returns are salable. But when the individual packages have been damaged, we toss them. Since product is put into those individual packages as part of manufacturing, it's not considered worth it to try to salvage them. It would cost more to salvage them in manufacturing than whatever we lose when we scrap them."

"Anything else?"

"Not that I can think of at the moment," replied Rich.

With a look of relief, Marcella thanked Rich for all his help and let him return to the warehouse. She looked at her notes and sighed as she thought, *How am I ever going to find a way to account for all this stuff?*

Chapter 8

About a week after her meeting with Rich, Marcella got an unexpected phone call. It was Caroline Perry, her former classmate.

"Hey, Marcella! It's Caroline. How's it going?" she asked.

After exchanging news about their families and personal lives, Marcella said, "I'm sure you didn't call me at work for a personal chat. What's up?"

"As I recall, when I saw you at the IMA meeting a couple of months ago, you were asking about models. I'm afraid I wasn't any help to you then, but while I was rummaging around in my dad's library last weekend, I think I found something that might provide some insight."

"Great! What have you got?"

"I probably never mentioned it, but my dad used to teach managerial economics at the university. His library has a lot of old books about decision-making and economics, most of them pretty boring, but I found one by a guy named Oxenfeldt that has a whole section on models. It's actually pretty interesting."

"That's great! Tell me more," Marcella said hopefully.

"Oxenfeldt says that models are 'simplified replications of reality.' That they express what we mean when we say that we know how something works. He says that the chief characteristics of models are that they simplify complex reality by stripping away the nonessential elements, including the essential elements, and understanding the relationships among those essential elements. He goes on to say that the main purpose of models is to make clear something that is complicated and that the value of a model depends upon the extent to which it increases our understanding."

"This sounds a lot like what the Major told me," interrupted Marcella.

"Who told you?"

"The Major. The old guy who comes to most of our IMA meetings and just listens."

"Oh, him. I didn't know he had a name," said Caroline, laughing. "And you talked to him?"

Marcella related how she had come to have a couple of conversations with the Major before asking, "Anything else interesting in the book?"

"Oh yes! He said that contrary to common belief, there is no such thing as *the* cost of anything. He even put a dig in at accountants, saying that accountants calculate costs in a particular way that serves their own purpose, but the needs of an executive making decisions are different from those of accountants.

"He also emphasized it was an unpleasant fact of life that executives' measurements of costs will never be exact, but that it's okay because it isn't necessary that they know their decision costs precisely. They must do the best they can under the circumstances. Decision-makers must understand what costs are relevant and then settle for estimates that are 'good enough' for the decision at hand. In his view, it would be foolhardy to pursue the goal of complete precision in costing.

"There was one statement in particular that I found interesting. I've got it written down here. It says, 'An error in estimating the magnitude of an effect usually is far less serious than mistakes due to wholly overlooked consequences.'"

"What do you suppose that means?" asked Marcella.

Caroline responded, "I take it to mean that if a factor is important in making a decision, you're better off estimating the effect of that factor, even if that estimate is somewhat questionable, than ignoring the factor altogether. If something is important, approximating is better than omitting.

"By the way," she continued, "I smuggled the book out of my dad's library. I'll bring it along to our next IMA meeting and let you borrow it for a while. He won't even notice it's gone. There was a lot of dust on it when I took it from the shelf."

"Thanks!" replied Marcella, "I look forward to reading it."

The conversation ended, and Marcella got back to the monthly routine that is the responsibility of every controller.

Chapter 9

The next Monday morning rolled around and Alex made his regular stop by Marcella's office. He was in an excellent mood. The weather had been great, and he must have had a good weekend on the links.

"Broke 80 both days," he bragged as he sat down. "Even won $20 from our friend Papasifakis. After I shot a 78 on Saturday, he didn't think I could break 80 again on Sunday. I even got the old cheapskate to pick up the tab for lunch in the clubhouse afterward. Yes, all in all, a good weekend. By the way, how's the warehouse model coming? Made any progress?"

Marcella shifted a little uneasily in her chair. "Yes and no," she replied. "I gathered a lot more details from Rich, but I'm still having trouble imagining how to put them together into a model that would cover everything but still be practical enough to put into practice. Everything I think of seems way too complex and cumbersome."

"I'm sure you'll come up with something. You'll become the Isaac Newton of warehouse accounting."

They both laughed.

"Now that I know more details, I'm hoping I can get some more specific advice from the Major when I seem him next week."

"Are you sure he'll be there?"

"I sure hope so. I'm pretty sure he has an answer to the problem, but he wants me to come up with one myself. The more I think about his questions and the nuggets of wisdom he drops, the closer I feel I am to understanding where he's trying to lead me. But I'm not there yet. My friend Caroline has also found a book she's going to lend me that talks about models, costs, and decision-making. She'll be at next week's meeting. I hope her book will help me as well."

Alex looked pleased. "I'm sure you've made more progress than you think you have. Your brain's gray cells are working in ways they've never worked before. That's very encouraging."

Chapter 10

Caroline was waiting for Marcella outside of Kingsley Arms the evening of the next IMA dinner. Under her arm was the book *Cost-Benefit Analysis for Executive Decision Making: The Danger of Plain Common Sense,* by Alfred Oxenfeldt.

"How did you even happen to pick out this book?" asked Marcella as Caroline handed her the volume. "The title sounds awful dry and boring."

"I don't know," she replied, "probably because the title was less dry and boring than the other books in Dad's library, and when I flipped it open, it didn't have a lot of complicated formulas and graphs. It also had what looked like scripts of conversations between people instead of just a long-winded, academic discourse. I thought that might make it interesting."

"Did it?"

"Yeah, it did. I think you'll find it a pretty easy read. I hope it helps with your challenge."

Marcella grinned. "Me too. I need all the help I can get."

The two headed into the meeting, mixed with friends, heard a talk about accounting foozles and frauds, and had a more-than-acceptable dinner. The Kingsley always put out a pretty good spread for the IMA group. Probably because it has been such a long-time, reliable customer. Nine meetings per year for a couple of decades makes for a good customer.

As the meeting wound down, Marcella looked for the Major. She had seen him during the presentation but had lost track of him afterwards. Finally, she saw him looking through the meeting room's door, motioning to her.

"Mrs. DeCou," he said, "I've got our table ready in the lounge and your Chardonnay waiting for you." Looking at the book in her hand, he added, "I see you've got a copy of Oxenfeldt's book with you. I found that book very insightful when I read it in the 1970s. What do you think of it?"

"Actually, I've just gotten it from my friend Caroline. She found it in her dad's library and thought I might find it useful. She did tell me about some of the ideas she found in it, and some of them sound a lot like you."

"Yes, Oxenfeldt was an excellent managerial economist, and many of the ideas he espoused are very relevant, I might even say powerful, for an accountant who hopes to provide value to his or her organization. We probably sound the same on some issues," he said with a smile, "because great minds think alike. I believe this book as well as the John Maurice Clark book that I mentioned to you last month should be 'must reading' for all management accountants.

"Now tell me," he continued, "how is your modeling project going?"

"I sense that I'm still wallowing around in all the information and ideas I've collected these past two months. I see some kind of foggy vision of what I'm after, but it's not clear enough yet to describe."

"I think you can call that progress."

"You think so?"

"Yes. I don't know exactly what you're thinking, but you're not processing the information the same way you would have two months ago. You're not thinking like a garden-variety accountant. That might have been the biggest hurdle you had to overcome. You've climbed outside of the box."

"How do you know that?"

"Because you haven't grabbed some off-the-shelf, rules-based accounting solution. You're wallowing around, as you call it, because you're searching for a solution that fits the facts, not one that fits the rules."

"That I am," Marcella responded, "and I can tell you, it sure ain't easy."

"It'll get easier. The fog will slowly clear, and a fundamentally sound model for assigning your warehouse's costs to customers with evolve."

"I hope so," said Marcella with a sigh. She then proceeded to tell the Major of the new things she had learned from Rich about the warehouse's operation.

"So let me sum this up to make sure I understand," the Major said as she finished her summary. "The people working in your warehouse store products, pick orders, consolidate orders, and prepare them for shipment. They also handle returned goods. Does that sum it up?"

"That's it in a nutshell."

The Major thought for a moment and then asked, "What is the ratio of people you have working in the warehouse to people you have working in the manufacturing facility? Just an approximation."

"I'd say it's about three or four people in manufacturing for every one person in the warehouse," answered Marcella.

"So roughly speaking, when you exclude management, technical, and administrative personnel, warehouse activities represent 20-25% of the work being done at PlumbCo. Does that sound right?"

"Yeah, that's about right. If you look at all the non-office-type work being done, around a quarter of it is in the warehouse."

"Now imagine that you didn't manufacture your products but purchased them instead. If that were the case, you'd have no manufacturing. All of your non-office-types would be working in the warehouse."

"Of course," replied Marcella. She caught herself, however, when she began to wonder why the Major was heading off on what appeared to be another of his tangents. After their first two sessions together, she was confident there was a lesson of some sort coming, and she had to stay mentally alert to gather it all in.

"If there weren't any manufacturing, do you think the warehouse costing model you'd create would be the same as it would be if you had manufacturing?"

"My immediate answer would be 'yes,' but I have the feeling that the correct answer is 'no.'"

"And why do you suspect the answer should be 'no'?"

"Because I think I'm catching on to your modus operandi. The obvious answer is probably wrong."

"If you didn't have manufacturing, what percentage of your business would the warehouse's cost model cover?"

"All of it, I guess."

"But you do have manufacturing, and it involves four to five times more workers than warehousing. So what percentage of your business activities will it actually cover?"

"A quarter or less of them."

"If a cost model is designed to cover a quarter of your activities, do you think it has to attain the same level of accuracy as one designed to cover all of your activities?"

"Probably not."

"Because?"

Marcella sat silently for a few minutes and sipped on her drink, deep in thought, with her eyes half shut. The Major said nothing as he watched her. After what seemed to be an eternity, her expression suddenly transformed into one of discovery.

"Assuming that our manufacturing model properly assigns manufacturing's costs to the products," she posited, "three-quarters of our activities are already being assigned properly to the customers who buy them. A 10% error in assigning the warehousing costs to customers would only result in a 2–2½% error in costs assigned to the customer. If we were just a warehouse, it would result in a 10% error. I would think that a model that covers everything you do would need to result in a greater degree of accuracy than one that covers only a quarter of what you do."

"Well played!" exclaimed the Major with a look of triumph on his face. "Another way to look at it is that you want a model that covers everything you do to be quite accurate, whereas a model that only covers a fraction of what you do need only be 'not wrong.' Materiality plays an important role in designing your model."

"So you're saying that my model of warehousing doesn't need to be all that complex?"

"Only complex enough to provide management with a depiction of reality that's accurate enough for their decision-making needs. If they feel the need to know each customer's profitability within tenths of a percent, the model needs to be pretty complex, and the system to implement it will probably very cumbersome. If, on the other hand, they want to understand how a customer's ordering practices impact its profitability and have measures of that impact that are 'not wrong,' the model can be much simpler. It still needs to reflect economic realities, mind you, but it doesn't need to chase minutiae or split hairs."

"That's very helpful," said Marcella, "although at the moment, I'm not sure how I would structure either the complex or simple model."

The Major thought for a moment and then asked, "Does your family have any pets?"

"Sure. We have a dog."

"No cats?"

"No, just a dog."

"Did you ever have any cats?"

"No. But when I was a kid, we had a family cat."

"Excellent! You do have experience with both dogs and cats."

I wonder where this is going, thought Marcella. But by now, she knew that the Major didn't go off topic in these conversations; he must be up to something.

"Tell me," the Major continued, "which of the two types of pets requires more care and maintenance: a dog or a cat?"

Marcella didn't hesitate. "Oh, a dog, by far. You've got to let them in and out of the house constantly, take them for walks, clean up their 'business,' and do all sorts of things. Cats, on the other hand, take care of themselves. Just put some food out for them, and clean the litter box a couple of times a week."

"Now, let's suppose you're in the pet-boarding business. You take care of customers' dogs and cats while the owners are away for an extended period. It costs you $120,000 per year to operate your business, and you provide 4,000 boarding days per year. That works out to $30 per animal per day boarded. Each dog costs you $30 per day, and each cat costs you $30 per day. Does that make sense to you?"

"Not really," replied Marcella. "I would think that with the higher care and maintenance required for dogs, they would be more costly per day."

"And cats would be less costly?"

"Of course. If the dogs were more costly than $30 per day, the cats would be less costly."

"Assuming that those 4,000 boarding days are split evenly between dogs and cats, can you envision a simple model that would allow you to differentiate the cost of pet care between the two?"

Marcella sat quietly thinking for a few minutes.

"Think weights," interrupted the Major.

"Weights?" replied Marcella quite puzzled. "You mean the weight of the animal?"

"No," laughed the Major. "Weights as in relative levels of effort. If a cat requires one unit of care per day, how many units per day does a dog require?"

"Oh, I think I see. If a dog requires twice the amount of care per day as a cat, it would have two 'care units' for every one 'care unit' required by a cat."

"That's right. Now how can you incorporate that into a model?"

Marcella didn't hesitate this time. "I could create a model that measures the cost of a care unit. A cat would get one care unit of cost per day and a dog would have two care units."

"Go on. Use your model to calculate the daily costs in my example."

"Let's see: 2,000 cat days would amount to 2,000 care units; 2,000 dog days would result in 4,000 care units. That totals 6,000 care units. Divided into the $120,000 annual cost means each care unit costs $20. So each cat day costs $20 and each dog day $40."

"So if you charged $36 per boarding day, what would that mean?"

"I'd be losing money on dogs and making a ridiculous profit on cats."

"Any other insights?"

Marcella thought for a few moments. "If my cost structure is like my competitors, I'd probably become pretty non-competitive on cats but attract a lot of dog business. I should probably reconsider my pricing policies."

"That's good. Anything else?"

"If I can't land dog business at the higher price, I know I must find ways to reduce the daily cost of caring for dogs below $40 if I'm to stay in business."

"That's good. You're not only measuring costs more accurately, you're gaining insights that can help you better manage your business. But tell me this: Do you think the cost is actually the same for all dogs and for all cats? Do some dogs really cost more than $40 per day and some less? Do some cats cost more than $20 daily and some less?"

"Of course they're not all the same."

"Does it matter?"

Again, Marcella thought for a few moments before answering. "Probably not. I've taken care of the big discrepancy in care for the two animals, but an error within each category would most likely be immaterial."

Marcella's cell phone rang. She was pretty late, and her family was checking in to make sure she was okay.

"We'd better call it a day," suggested the Major.

"You're probably right," replied Marcella. "You'll be here next month, won't you?"

"That's the plan," said the Major and then added, "Don't forget about the pet-boarding business while designing your warehousing model."

Before Marcella could respond, the Major was out the door and headed for the parking lot.

Chapter 11

A lex was in a somber mood when he arrived in Marcella's office the following Monday. It had rained all weekend and made it impossible for him to get in a single round of golf.

"Without golf, what did you do with your time all weekend?" inquired Marcella. She was obviously getting more comfortable having these conversations with her boss.

"Oh, we sat in the clubhouse, had lunch, and watched golf on television. Thank God for the Golf Channel. If it weren't for the Golf Channel, I might have wound up playing cards ... and I hate playing cards. What'd you do?"

"Caught up on some of the household chores and even had some time left over to get into this book my friend Caroline purloined from her father's library." She spun the book around on her desk so that the title faced the Admiral.

"Ouch!" he said. "Just the title of that book is a bit painful. Did you make it past the table of contents?"

"Quite a bit past it. Oxenfeldt was a management economist, not an accountant, and his concerns were about cost information for management decisions, not cost information for accounting. The beginning of the book talks a lot about the importance of models in decision-making, the impact our models of reality have on our lives, and what makes for a valid model. It wasn't only quite interesting, it was quite relevant to our warehousing model problem and pointed out many of the same issues the Major has discussed during our conversations."

"Oh yeah, the Major. Have you seen him lately?"

"Just last week. After our IMA meeting, as usual."

"Did he turn on any new light bulbs?"

"As a matter of fact, he did. He walked me through an exercise about a pet-boarding business that gave me a few ideas to try out on Rich later this week."

"A pet-boarding business?"

"Yes, a pet-boarding business."

"I don't think I'll ask you to explain. If you think it gave you some ideas that'll help in modeling our warehouse, that's good enough for me.

"By the way, while Theron Papasifakis and I were watching golf on Saturday, he made a rather unflattering crack about accountants."

Marcella sighed. It hadn't taken long for her to arrive at the conclusion that Mr. Papasifakis wasn't a big fan of accountants. "And that crack was?" she responded.

"He said that if accountants were doctors, we'd still be making appointments to have leeches applied and get ourselves bled so we could balance our humors."

"Am I supposed to respond to that?"

"No. Not really. I just thought you'd be interested." After a pause, Alex added with a smile, "I did tell him that I thought my controller was an exception."

Marcella blushed at the backhanded compliment.

"You'll be meeting with Rich soon, then?"

"Yes, tomorrow afternoon."

"Great," replied Alex. "Now let's get down to the forecast for the rest of the month."

Chapter 12

Rich Vivian showed up at Marcella's office at 2:00 sharp. Marcella noticed that, in addition to being on time, Rich had a look of excited anticipation. Quite unlike the look of mild annoyance he had when she visited with him in the plant a few weeks earlier.

"You ready to rock 'n roll?" he asked as he sat down across from her.

"Sure am," she replied.

"Then how do we start?"

After looking at her notes for a few moments, Marcella said, "Let's take each of the key activities your staff does, one by one, and think of how they may be different for different customers or products. We'll start with receiving product from manufacturing and putting it away."

"Okay." Rich leaned forward in his seat.

"Approximately what percentage of the warehousing crew's work is involved in receiving and putting away the product? You don't need to be precise, just a ballpark figure."

"Oh, maybe 5%. It's not really a lot of time."

"Does each pallet of product take about the same amount of time to put away?"

"Yeah, I'd say that's true. It varies a little, but not much."

"But each pallet doesn't contain the same amount of product, does it?"

"No. There might be 200 of the larger parts on a pallet and 500 of the smaller ones."

"So in that case, at least in theory, each of the larger parts costs more to put away than each of the smaller parts."

"How's that?"

"Well, just for argument's sake, let's say putting away a pallet costs $10. That would mean it costs five cents each to put away larger items but only two cents each to put away smaller ones."

"That true, but I doubt if it costs $10 to put away a pallet."

"I agree. My intuition tells me that it'll be less. But in that case, the difference in cost between the larger and smaller quantities would be even less that the three cents in my example. If putting a pallet away costs only $5, the difference would be a cent and a half."

"If you say so." Rich was not as quick as Marcella with his math.

"I'd say that, due to the small numbers involved, we'd be safe in assuming that each unit of product costs about the same to put away. There wouldn't be much value in trying to be any more accurate than that," concluded Marcella.

"Sounds reasonable."

––––––––––––

"Now, once the goods are put away, they sit in inventory for a while. Some for a long time and some for a short time."

Rich smiled and said, "Or another way of looking at it, each product rents its space in its cube, or cubes, for a different period of time."

"That's good," laughed Marcella. "As I recall, each product has its own assigned cube or cubes."

"Correct."

"So a particular product rents an apartment, some one room and some multiple rooms, for a given period of time. If we know the cost of renting a cube for a year, we can figure out the cost of storing the products that occupy that cube for the year; excluding the cost of money, of course. We're going to ignore the cost of money for this pass at the problem."

"I'm with you so far."

"If we know how many units of product passed through the apartment during a given year, we can determine a cost per unit of product for storage. So if a cube costs $500 per year and 2,000 parts pass through that cube, each part will cost 25 cents to store. If 5,000 parts pass through, it'll cost a dime."

"So the way of measuring storage cost would be to divide each product's annual volume into its annual cube-rental cost," interjected Rich.

"That's right," replied Marcella. "But we have to keep materiality in mind."

"We have to keep what in mind?"

"Materiality. Sort of like we did with put-away. We need to ask ourselves if the benefit is worth the effort to have that level of accuracy. Or is there another, less complex, way that would still take the varying storage costs into account and provide us with information that is 'accurate enough' without so many calculations? Are the dollars we're talking about worth the effort?"

"You mean 'Is the climb worth the view?'"

"That's it exactly. Where'd you pick up that expression anyway?"

"I don't really remember. I heard it somewhere once and it popped into my head while you were talking. What other way could there be for doing the calculation?"

"Well, I don't know if this is where we'll go, but one simpler alternative occurred to me. We've already segregated our inventory into three categories for picking purposes based on product popularity, haven't we?"

"I can see you paid attention during our earlier meeting," laughed Rich. "You're right."

"Then what if we determined the average product volume in each of those three categories and used those volumes to come up with an average storage cost per product for each of the three categories?" As Marcella finished, another thought occurred to her. "Or maybe we could determine the total cost of cube rental for each of those categories and divide by the total volume in each category to arrive at the three storage costs per unit of product?"

"You're going too fast for me." Rich looked like he was actually enjoying himself.

"That's okay. The point is that we have some options. Once we see what kind of dollars we're talking about, we can figure out what route to take on storage costs."

"Sounds good to me. Where to now?"

"I think order entry is next," replied Marcella as she shuffled through her notes. "It looks like there are three or four categories of orders: electronic, fax or mail, and telephone. It's four if we treat fax and mail as separate categories, and it's three if we put them together. Does that sound right?'

"Yup."

"And all of the work done in entering the orders is done by customer service?"

"Yeah. They handle all three or four types of incoming orders."

"I would imagine that an incoming electronic order would require the least amount of customer service's time, and a telephone order would take the most time." As she spoke, her own words triggered a mental image of the pet-boarding business the Major had talked about at the last IMA meeting.

"Oh yes, telephone orders are a pain. I would guess that they take 8–10 times more effort to process than an electronic order."

"And where would fax and mail orders rank on the customer service effort meter?"

"Somewhere in between. Maybe about halfway in between."

"How about the difference in effort required to process fax versus mail orders?"

"It's really not very different. You get one in the mail and the other comes off the fax machine. From that point on, they're really the same."

"So we can treat them the same? Just one category for both?"

"Works for me."

Marcella thought for a few moments and then said, "You indicated that a telephone order probably requires 8-10 times more work for customer service than does an electronic order. Is that right?"

"That's right."

"Let's pick 8 as the number. If we say that a telephone order is 8 times more work than an electronic order, then what multiplier would we use to reflect the difference between an electronic order and a mail or fax order?"

"Uh, come again?" Rich had gotten a bit lost at that last turn.

"How many times more work is there in customer service to handle a telephone order versus an electronic order? Think 'effort units.' If handling an electronic order requires 1 effort unit and handling a telephone order requires 8 effort units, then how many effort units are required to handle a mail or fax order?"

Rich looked like he understood this time. His eyes narrowed while he pondered the question. Finally he answered, "I'd say it's about halfway in between: 4. Yes, 4 effort units would be about right."

"Good," replied Marcella with a look of satisfaction. She was rather surprised at how much she was enjoying this exercise. "Let me try some math on you again."

"Oh, great!" sighed Rich, "More math."

"Rich, math is an occupational hazard for a manager. You can't avoid it. The example of products renting apartment space wasn't too complicated, was it?"

"No, I guess not. Try me."

"Okay." Marcella came around to Rich's side of the desk with her pad and began writing down numbers. "Let's say we get 5,000 electronic orders, 2,000 mail/fax orders, and 1,000 telephone orders annually."

"We get a lot more than that."

"I know that. This is just an example. You wanted me to keep the math simple, right?"

"Okay. Carry on, Professor."

"Now let's turn these order counts into measurements of work required to process the orders, using the effort units we talked about."

"How do we do that?"

"It's actually pretty simple. We multiply each order category's count by the effort units you estimated for that category's transactions. The 1,000 telephone orders are multiplied by their 8 effort units, for a total of 8,000. The 2,000 mail/fax orders are multiplied by their 4 effort units, for a total of 8,000: the same total effort as the telephone orders. This is just an example, but if these were real numbers, it would tell us that we spend the same amount of time processing 1,000 telephone orders as we do processing 2,000 mail/fax orders. Electronic orders are our base for determining effort units, so we multiply the 5,000 electronic orders by their effort unit of 1, for a total of 5,000."

"I'm following so far, but what does it tell us?"

"If we add the three totals together, it says that customer service provides a total of 21,000 effort units annually. But the numbers also tell us what percentage of this effort relates to each of our three order categories: 8,000—or 38% of the 21,000 effort units—relate to telephone orders. The same holds true for mail/fax orders: 38% of customer service's effort relates to them. The balance of 24% relates to the electronic orders. Now, if we assume that customer service costs us $100,000 per year—"

"Wait! Wait! Let me do this!" interjected Rich. "I think I see where we're going."

"Okay, you take the controls," laughed Marcella.

"If customer service costs $100,000 per year, and 38% of its effort is spent processing 1,000 telephone orders, the cost per telephone order is $38 each. Am I on track?"

"So far, so good."

"We spend the same amount processing mail/fax orders, but because there are twice as many of them, the cost would only be $19 each."

"You're on a roll, Rich!"

"So 24% of the cost, or $24,000, is spent to process 5,000 electronic orders. That's only $4.80 per order. We've got a cost of processing each type of order."

"You nailed it!" exclaimed Marcella. They were both laughing. "But don't get too carried away, this was just an example of how we could do it. What do you think? Is a process such as the one we just went through a realistic and practical way to do this?"

"I like it. And I think I actually understand it. Even the math part. If we can do something like this for real, it'd be great information. I know the numbers we used are just made up, but I always suspected we might not be making much money, or maybe even losing money, on the small orders we get over the phone. Being able to measure this stuff would be great."

"Well, we've still got a way to go. We'd better get on to the next step."

"Picking," interjected Rich. "This should be interesting."

"As I recall, orders are consolidated into pick lists that are more efficient to pick than individual orders. Although this is undoubtedly a solid idea, it does complicate linking the picking activity's costs to customers because it means a picker can be working on a list that includes multiple orders from multiple customers. Keeping track of a picker's time as he or she goes from location to location isn't practical, and even if it were, it wouldn't make any sense. Travel time from one cube to another would depend on where the cube that preceded it on the pick list was located. Not only that, but two customers on a pick list could be buying the same part number, so one trip to a cube could be serving two customers. Linking picking costs to customers is certainly not very straightforward or obvious. You got any ideas?"

"You're right about the process, but you're wrong if you think I've got a clue about how to track these costs to a customer. Would some kind of effort unit approach like we used for order entry work here?" Rich was actually trying to be helpful.

Marcella had wondered the same thing. Maybe there was a way to use the Major's pet-boarding methodology here as well. "Let's just think out loud for a while," she suggested. "Maybe something one of us says will generate the spark of an idea."

"Okay, you start," said Rich.

"Thanks!" replied Marcella. "Let's see ..." She hesitated for a few moments. "Our objective here is to link the cost of picking orders to customers."

"So far, so good."

"But figuring out and assigning the picking cost each time a picker makes a circuit to complete his or her pick list appears to be impractical and, at least as far as my brain goes, probably impossible."

"Couldn't agree more."

"The question then becomes, 'Can we accomplish our objective without the ability to make such a measurement?'" Marcella paused again. "When you think about it," she suddenly added, "we're not trying to link picking costs to each shipment we make to a customer, but to the business we do with each customer over time. What we're really trying to do is distribute the cost of all of our picking activities to the customers we've served during some period of time. Let's say over the course of a year. We sold so much to a customer and earned a margin on those sales during a year, but now we want to know how much our picking efforts ate into those margins. If we frame our objective in those terms, we might be able to come up with a solution.

"For example," she continued, "if one customer bought 10 of the same items located near the shipping area each month, the picking costs would be pretty low. On the other hand, if another customer bought 1 of 10 different items located far from the shipping area, the costs would be much higher. The first customer's parts would require only a short trip and one stop each month. The second customer's parts would require a long trip and 10 stops."

"But we don't pick one order at a time," objected Rich. "Orders are combined on a pick list, and the pickers are picking multiple orders all at once."

"I'm not sure that matters for our reframed objective. We're looking for picking effort over time, not for an individual order. The first customer's ordering behavior over time will require less picking effort than does the second customer's behavior. As I recall, it's the cube-to-cube movement that takes up most of the pickers' time. On average, moving to a nearby cube will be less costly than going to a distant cube."

"Okay. Where does that put us?"

"It puts us at your ABC system for storing the product based on its popularity. Let's assume each line item on an order requires a move from one location to another. I know that's not always true, you combine orders on a pick list, but it's probably true in a majority of cases. Assume that we could come up with the average cost per line item for picking an "A" item, a "B" item, and a "C" item. The distance of the part from the shipping area would be the determining factor."

Marcella grabbed her pencil and paper again. "Let's say we spend $500,000 on picking each year." She paused. "Remember these are just numbers to make a point, not our actual numbers. Then let's say we pick 50,000 line items from Group A, then 20,000 from Group B, and 10,000 from Group C. How much more time do you think it would take to pick a Group B line item than a Group A line item?"

"You mean how many minutes?" asked Rich.

"No. In relation to a trip to Group A. Would it be twice as much time? Half again as much time? Just give me an educated guess."

"I'd say half again as much time. Not much more than that."

"Great. Now how much more time than Group A to get to Group C?"

"Oh, probably twice as much time."

"Okay. Let me crunch a few numbers." Marcella reached for her calculator, put her head down, and began writing. After a few minutes, she said, "Here," and showed Rich her calculations:

Group	Line Items	Weight	Weighted Line Items	Pct	Dollars	Cost per Line Item
Group A	50,000	1.0	50,000	50.0%	$250,000	$5.00
Group B	20,000	1.5	30,000	30.0%	$150,000	$7.50
Group C	10,000	2.0	20,000	20.0%	$100,000	$10.00
Totals	80,000		100,000	100.0%	$500,000	

"If we multiply each group's line items by the weight—which is the relative time you gave me—we come up with weighted line items. These weighted line items represent the relative effort spent in picking each group's line items. We turn that into percentages and apply them to the total cost of picking activities to assign picking costs to each group. We can then come up with a picking cost per line item." Marcella was quite pleased with herself and thought the Major would be impressed as well at her use of his pet-boarding example.

Rich studied her chart and said, "So this says picking a line item in Group A would cost $5 while picking one in Group C would cost $10. Right?"

"That's right. Based on your time estimates, it would take twice as much time and thereby cost twice as much."

"Interesting."

"Let's apply it to the two examples I used earlier. The first customer would require that we pick 12 Group A line items per year, for a total of $60. The second customer would require us to pick 120 Group C line items per year, for a total of $1,200."

"Wow! That's quite a difference!" interjected Rich. "Who'd have ever thought—"

"Remember," Marcella interrupted, "this is just an example I made up, not our real situation. The two customers were at two extremes and probably not like any of our customers. But the basic concept, does it make sense to you?"

Rich thought for a few moments and said, "I like it. And I think it's something we could actually do. Our system already tracks line items by customers, and if the IT folks can work in a weight for each product based on its inventory grouping, then we could do this within the existing system."

"Then let's go with it for now. We've still got to address shipping."

"Oh yeah," sighed Rich, "I was hoping we were done."

"I think we're getting this down. I hope shipping won't take us long." Marcella shuffled through her notes again. "It looks like there are four issues in shipping. First, they have to sort and box up any loose items delivered to their area. Second, boxed items are prepared for shipment via the daily UPS pickup. Third, large orders are palletized, shrink-wrapped, and loaded onto the trailer. Finally, we've got the returns and restocks. Those last items also include some effort from receiving and the cost of the product we scrap."

"That's right," said Rich, "and don't forget that boxed items incur the cost of the box itself, and palletized shipments incur the cost of the pallet, shrink-wrap, and strapping. There's also the cost of operating the shrink-wrap machine to consider."

"Darn you!" responded Marcella.

"What'd I do?" reacted Rich.

"You messed up my thinking. I was thinking we could take the cost of shipping activities and assign it to the four types of activities using the weighting method we used earlier. You know, transaction count times the relative effort expended on each of the four activities. But costs like boxes, pallets, and shrink-wrap machines would screw that all up. They each relate to only one of the four activities. It doesn't seem logical to put them into the pool of shipping activity costs and distribute them on effort."

"Oh yeah. I see the problem," was Rich's reply.

They both sat silent for a while until Marcella's face suddenly lit up. "I know what we can do," she said.

"What's that?"

"We can still take the cost of shipping activities without including the boxes, pallets, and the like and distribute it using our weighting process. We can then add the cost of those items to the distributed activity cost before calculating the cost per transaction."

"Huh?"

"It's actually pretty simple. Why don't you go get a cup of coffee while I do a little math to come up with an example?"

"Your wish is my command," laughed Rich.

Marcella went back to work scribbling on her pad and pounding on her calculator. About 15 minutes later, she had come up with her example. Rich returned a few minutes later.

"Check this out," she said and turned her sheet around so Rich could read it.

Activity	Transactions	Weight	Weighted Transactions	Pct	Activity Dollars	Assigned Cost	Revised Dollars	Cost per Transaction
Box Loose Orders	2,500	1.0	2,500	8.0%	$20,000	$0	$20,000	$8.00
Box Shipments	7,500	1.0	7,500	24.0%	$60,000	$7,500	$67,500	$9.00
Pallet Shipments	5,000	4.0	20,000	64.0%	$160,000	$20,000	$180,000	$36.00
Return/Restocks	1,250	1.0	1,250	4.0%	$10,000	$2,500	$12,500	$10.00
Totals	16,250		31,250	100.0%	$250,000	$30,000	$280,000	

"Assuming we spend $250,000 on shipping activities," she explained, "we can distribute the cost to each of the four transaction types using the weighting process. Remember these are made-up numbers to explain the concept. No real numbers."

"Yeah, yeah. I understand. You don't have to explain that to me anymore," replied Rich.

"Okay. Once we've distributed the activity costs, we can add the cost of boxes to 'box shipments,' the cost of pallets, shrink-wrap, banding, and the shrink-wrap machine to 'pallet shipments,' and the cost of scrapped product to 'returns/restocks.' After adding them to the activity cost, we can then divide by the number of transactions and come up with a cost per transaction."

"Ingenious." Rich liked the idea. "But won't the cost be different if we scrap a return than if we can restock one?"

"That's true. But from a big-picture standpoint, I figure the amounts involved will be too small to worry about. If, in my example, one turned out to be $8 and the other $12, it wouldn't have a big impact on our understanding of customer profitability. The fact that they're returning product would be the main issue, and we've got that covered.

"Let's create a customer and calculate the shipping cost required to support their sales." She reached for her pad and calculator again.

"Should I leave you alone again?" Rich laughed.

"No. Just sit there and be quiet for a minute or two."

Rich complied and in a couple of minutes, Marcella was done with her calculations.

"I just created a couple of customers. To one, we sold 20 boxes of loose parts and made a total of 50 box shipments and 100 pallet shipments. That customer also had 5 returns. That works out to a shipping cost of $4,260 to support that customer's sales. The other customer bought the same volume product but always in smaller quantities. We had to fill 200 boxes with loose parts and shipped a total of 500 boxes. Their shipping costs amount to $6,150. Pretty slick, eh?"

"That's one way to put it," said Rich. "Are we done now?"

"You sound like my kids. 'Are we there yet?' And yes, I think we're done for now. I'll summarize all this and present it to Alex. I'm anxious to see what he thinks. You want to be there when I explain it to him?"

"You want me there?" Rich was surprised to be invited to a meeting with the boss. He had never been asked to a meeting with the CEO before.

"Of course! This is as much yours as it is mine."

"Then let me know when it is, and I'll be there."

Rich headed back to the warehouse feeling a little more appreciated than he had ever been before, and Marcella started putting together her summary while everything was fresh in her mind. She was also wondering what Alex—and the Major—would think of her efforts.

Chapter 13

M arcella was ready for Alex when he appeared in her office the following Monday morning. She had told Rich to stop by her office earlier so both of them were there when Alex arrived. After discussing the social and golfing events of the weekend, Marcella slipped a piece of paper across her desk so Alex could reach it and said, "Rich and I came up with some ideas for costing the warehouse."

"Great!" replied Alex. "What have you got?"

"I've summarized them in the table in front of you."

Warehouse Activity		Cost Assignment Basis		Cost Rate Measurement Calculation
Put-Away		Cost per unit		Total PA Cost/Total Units PA
Storage		Cost per Group A Unit		Group A Storage Cost/Cat A Units
		Cost per Group B Unit		Group B Storage Cost/Cat B Units
		Cost per Group C Unit		Group C Storage Cost/Cat C Units
Order		Telephone Orders		Weighted Cost per Order
		Mail/Fax Orders		Weighted Cost per Order
		Electronic orders		Weighted Cost per Order

Warehouse Activity		Cost Assignment Basis		Cost Rate Measurement Calculation
Picking		Cost per Group A Unit		Weighted Cost per Line Item
		Cost per Group B Unit		Weighted Cost per Line Item
		Cost per Group C Unit		Weighted Cost per Line Item
Shipping		Loose Order Shipment		Weighted Cost per Transaction (Box)
		Box Shipment		Weighted Cost per Transaction (Box)
		Pallet Shipment		Weighted Cost per Transaction (Pallet)
		Return/Restock		Weighted Cost per Transaction (Return)

Alex looked at Marcella's table for a few moments and said, "I think you'll have to explain this."

"Okay. First, we've broken down warehousing operations into five activities: Put-Away, Storage, Order Processing, Order Picking, and Shipping. The cost assignment bases describe the way we plan to assign each activity's cost to a customer. For example, for each unit it buys, a customer will be assigned a cost for its being put away and its storage. The put-away cost will be the same for each unit. We know the actual cost will be different for different products because warehousing puts away pallets, and not every pallet has the same number of units. But intuition tells us that the difference will not be significant enough to distort the total cost of serving a customer. We're following Oxenfeldt's Rule in this case."

"Oxenfeldt's Rule?" asked Alex.

"Yes, Oxenfeldt's Rule. You may remember that my friend Caroline Perry loaned me a book by a management economist named Alfred Oxenfeldt. In it, he says, 'An error in estimating the magnitude of an effect usually is far less serious than mistakes due to wholly overlooked consequences.' In other words, it's better to include an estimate of a factor, even if that estimate is not extremely accurate, than to leave that factor out altogether.

I figure that this is especially true in instances where it doesn't appear that the factor is critical. After we do the calculations, if we find that the amount involved isn't worth worrying about, we might bury the cost somewhere else."

"That sound right to you, Rich?" Alex wanted to get Rich involved in the discussion.

"Yes sir," replied Rich, "put-away only amounts to about 5% of what my people do, but it is one of the five categories of activities they perform. I agree with Marcella that it's important to include it in our model, but not worry too much about the preciseness of the measurement. Every unit will get a charge for being put away ... we won't be overlooking anything. If it turns out that put-away costs are more than 5% of our total work, we might reconsider, but for now I agree that this is the right way."

Alex was surprised at how much Rich seemed to have picked up on the idea, both from a cooperation and a comprehension standpoint. Marcella must have communicated with him effectively and got him to buy in to the process and feel himself a key member of the team.

"Sounds good." Alex interjected, "What about the second activity, storage?"

"In reality," began Marcella, "each product will have a different storage cost based on how many cubes it requires and the number of products that pass through that cube, or those cubes, annually. Measuring a storage cost for each product would most likely be much too cumbersome and probably unnecessary. On the other hand, intuition tells us that doing things the same way we did with put-away and having the same storage cost for each unit would be ignoring a factor that could be significant. We needed to somehow account for the difference between items that turn fairly quickly and therefore require little storage time per unit and those that turn slowly and require a lot of storage time. Fortunately, every product in our inventory has already been assigned to one of three "groups" based on how quickly it turns. Rich and I decided that the three rates we'd get by assigning storage cost to the three groups and dividing by each group's annual unit volume would enable us to differentiate storage costs between quick, average, and slow-moving products."

"It sounds like Oxenfeldt's Rule again," laughed Alex. "You took a factor into account with a reasonable estimate instead of omitting it because it was too cumbersome to calculate with great exactness."

"That's right," said Marcella. "I think that rule, or principle, is particularly powerful in areas like warehousing where it's impractical for workers to track their time. If these workers had to track their time, they'd be spending half of their working hours just tracking what they were doing."

"You can bet the farm on that," interjected Rich. "They'd be constantly switching customers or products to charge their time to."

"Next," Marcella continued, "we addressed order processing, our third activity. Orders come in over the phone, by mail, by fax, or electronically. Mail and fax orders require about the same amount of effort, so we combined them into one activity. Phone orders, on the other hand, take a great deal of time, and electronic orders take almost no time at all.

"We couldn't treat all orders as being the same (like we did with put-away), and breaking the activity costs into categories (like we did with storage) would seem to be impractical. With storage, we can physically identify the areas in which each of the three groups are stored and assign storage costs by square footage occupied. In customer service, however, individual workers handle all three kinds of orders as they arrive. They could be handling a phone order one minute and a mail order five minutes later. There is no simple way to break their costs into the three categories. It changes day-to-day, week-to-week, and month-to-month based on the kinds of orders received."

"I can see that would be pretty impractical," interjected Alex. "So how did you solve that problem?"

"As you may recall, the Major told me a story about the pet-boarding business."

"Oh, yes. And I told you not to bother to explain it to me."

"That's right."

"If it may be important," Alex added, "maybe I should ask you to tell me that story now." Marcella then went on to relate the Major's story. When she was finished, Alex said, "Okay. Now go ahead and tell me how you used that story in solving your order-processing challenge."

"I asked Rich to estimate the level of effort for each of the categories, using 1.0 as the effort level for electronic orders. In other words, if an electronic order takes 1.0 unit of effort, how many units would be required for the phone and mail/fax orders? He estimated that mail/fax orders take 4 times the effort and phone orders take 8 times the effort. Using his estimates, I put together this example to explain the calculation."

She passed another piece of paper to Alex's side of the desk. "Take a look at it."

Group	Orders	Weight	Weighted Orders	Pct	Dollars	Cost per Order
Phone	1,000	8.0	8,000	38.1%	$38,095	$38.10
Mail/Fax	2,000	4.0	8,000	38.1%	$38,095	$19.05
Electronic	5,000	1.0	5,000	23.8%	$23,810	$4.76
Totals	8,000		$21,000	100.0%	$100,000	

After examining Marcella's schedule for a few moments, Alex asked, "Does it really cost only $100,000 to process our orders?"

"Alex!" Marcella exclaimed, "it's an example. I made up all the numbers except Rich's effort weights to show how it works. The numbers aren't real."

Alex smiled and laughed. "I was just pulling your leg. I've noticed how irked you get when people don't pay attention to the point you're trying to make and just pay attention to the numbers themselves. Go ahead. I'll shut up."

Marcella then proceeded to explain the weighting process and how it arrives at three different order costs based on effort required.

Alex looked at Rich. "So it takes 8 times more work to process a phone order than an electronic order?"

"Sure does," replied Rich, "at least that much. An electronic order fits the description of 'untouched by human hands.' There's actually no physical work required to enter it. It's just 'eyeballed' by order entry to make sure there are no problems or issues. If there are, they call the customer for clarification. But that's the exception; 99% of the orders are fine. Mail and fax orders require that the order be entered into the computer system by the order-entry folks. That takes time. They also require the occasional follow-up phone call. Phone orders take not only the time to enter the order, but they almost always include a conversation with the customer to answer questions and confirm their information. I believe the three weights pretty much approximate the relative levels of effort."

"Now," Marcella reentered the conversation, "if all these numbers were true—which they aren't—and we had two customers who purchased the same products at the same price during the year, but one customer gave us one phone order per month and the other one electronic order per month, serving the customer making phone orders would cost us $400 more per year. Not an exact measurement, but one that is close enough to provide us insight into the two customers' real profitability. Another application of Oxenfeldt's Rule."

"I really like this so far," interjected Alex. "Keep going."

"Next comes order picking, our fourth activity. Rich and I figured that, over the long term, the time required for picking was a function of the item's distance from shipping. The cost of picking is mostly driven by moving from location to location. The time spent actually picking the item probably entails less than 20% of the pickers' time. Again, we're not trying to be exact, but provide insight into the cost of serving our customer, so we focused on the primary driver of picking cost, which is the movement from cube to cube. If you think about it, a picker must move from cube to cube for every line item on an order. Over time—and I want to emphasize the importance of the phrase 'over time'—picking items close to packing will take less time than those located far away. So we decided that the best method would be to compute a picking cost per line item."

"Why is the phrase 'over time' so important?" asked Alex.

Rich jumped in. "Because for any given order, the route taken by the picker will be different. Sometimes a line item located far from shipping will come after a line item located near shipping, requiring more travel time that it would have had it come after a line item for another item located far from shipping. The actual pick time for every line item will be different, depending on the other items in the order. Over time, however, we believe it's pretty safe to assume that items far from shipping will take more picking time than those near shipping."

"That makes sense to me," responded Alex.

Marcella resumed, "Fortunately, our three inventory groups already reflect the distance of the part from shipping. So we used those three groups as a basis for weighting the line items." She passed a copy of the example she had prepared for Rich to Alex.

"Great!" was Alex's response after studying the example. "I think we're getting to where we want to be. And now we've got shipping, right?"

"Correct," said Marcella. "Our fifth activity is shipping, and it presents the same problem as picking. The shippers are working on whatever types of shipments come along each day. It's impractical for them to track their time. So we used the same process as we did for picking, only we broke the shipments into categories based on time required to prepare the shipment.

"In discussing this with Rich, it became apparent that the major differences were between loose parts, boxes, and pallets. There is a complicating factor, however. Shipping also requires shipping materials: boxes, pallets, strapping, and the like. Fortunately, we can tell which type of shipment requires each of those items and can assign them to the appropriate category and incorporate them into the weighting process.

"There is also a second complicating factor: The shipping department handles returns. We figured that we should also include a category for handling returns so we can make sure we assign those costs to the right customers." She then passed the example she used earlier to Alex.

"Marcella," said Alex smiling, "I think you and Rich nailed it. This all looks like something we can do. Being exact in these areas is nigh on impossible, but exactness isn't what we need. We need insight into customer profitability, and this will no doubt provide that. Well done! Now who do you think should lead the effort to get it implemented?"

"I thought I would," she replied.

"You can give the implementation guidance, but I've got other things for you to do. How about Jim: Do you think he could lead the implementation?"

"Jim Stinson? He's pretty new. Do you think he's got the experience to do this?" James Stinson was a recent addition to Marcella's full-time staff. He had been an intern at PlumbCo while attending college, was hired immediately after graduation, and had been working there full time for about six months.

"As I recall," replied Alex, "he's pretty up-to-date on technology and worked closely with the IT folks on a lot of his projects while an intern. I'm sure he'll understand your design and be able to work well with the others we'll need to include on a project team. It'll also give him a chance to learn more about the nuances of our business. He appears to have a lot of potential and I'd put him to the test. You know Jim, don't you, Rich? What do you think of having him lead this implementation?"

Rich thought for a moment. "He did an excellent job helping us with some of our system issues while he was an intern. Everyone I talked with was impressed with his ability to grasp the issues and work with the various folks needed to get them solved. I could certainly work with him on this."

"That's great," said Marcella, "I'll bring him up to speed."

Alex looked at Marcella. "You and I can present this at our next staff meeting, and I will let everyone know how important this project is and that I'll be evaluating those involved on their ability to make it happen. In the meantime ..."

"In the meantime?"

"I've got something else for you to look into."

Oh, great! thought Marcella. *Here comes another project.* "What great issue would you like me to explore this time?" she asked.

"We had a meeting of the marketing folks last week, and several of them expressed concern over our competitiveness on some of our products. For whatever reason, it appears that we're more competitive on our larger products than on our smaller ones. No one can figure out why that might be. They're made in the same facility by the same people using the same processes."

"That is curious," she replied.

"I suspect it might have something to do with the way we determine the cost of those products. There might be something amiss in the way we assign manufacturing costs to individual products. What do you think?"

"Well, we assign costs the same way most manufacturers do: We track the direct labor to the part and assign overhead as a percentage of that direct labor."

"Do you think that accurately models the resources we use to produce a finished item?"

"Based on my recent experience with warehousing, I'm not sure. Let me look into it."

"Maybe you can bounce this off the Major. When will you see him again?"

"Our last meeting before summer break is next Tuesday. I hope he'll be there. I want to see what he thinks of what we've done with warehousing, and I'll see if he can give me any hints as to what to look for with this problem."

"Great!" said Alex. "I'd better get to my office and do some work." With that, he headed out the door.

Marcella and Rich looked at each other with satisfaction.

"I guess we nailed it," said Rich. He was pleased that his first real exposure to top management had been successful.

"Now we just have to make sure we nail the implementation as well," added Marcella.

"Don't worry," he said, "Jim and I will make sure it works. And thanks for letting me be involved in this. I really appreciate you including me in all of this." With that, he left Marcella's office and headed back to the warehouse.

Chapter 14

As was the case at the earlier meetings, Marcella didn't notice the Major until the monthly IMA meeting was winding down and everyone was packing up to leave. He was standing just outside the meeting-room door.

"Did you enjoy tonight's speaker?" he asked as she approached him.

"Not really," she answered. "I think I was too hyped up waiting to talk to you to pay much attention."

"Really? I can't remember anyone ever being 'hyped up' to talk with me before."

"I've got a lot to tell you. I think we've come up with an approach to costing our distribution activities."

The Major motioned toward the lounge and said, "Then let's order our drinks and find a spot to talk."

Once settled, Marcella handed the Major copies of her examples and went through the rationale for each element in the costing process she and Rich had developed. It took her almost a half hour. The Major sat expressionless while listening the entire time. When she was done, she looked up and said, "Well," she asked, "what do you think?"

A big smile grew on the Major's face, "Well done, Isaac Newton!" he exclaimed. "You created your own calculus for distribution. I was pretty sure you were up to it. What did your boss think?"

"Alex seemed pleased as well."

"So what are you going to do now? Will your new distribution costing methodology be implemented?"

"That's the next step. Alex wants me to oversee the implementation, but it will be spearheaded by a new member of my staff."

The Major looked a bit puzzled. "Just oversee the implementation? Why doesn't he have you heading it up?"

"He's given me another issue to explore."

"I think I like this Alex. What new issue?"

"Our marketing people told him that we're much more competitive on our larger products than on our smaller ones. He seems to think that it might have something to do with how we cost them, so he tasked me with looking into it."

The Major thought for a few moments. "As I recall," he said, "you charge direct labor directly to the product and then assign manufacturing overhead to it as a percentage of that labor. Is that right?"

"That's how we do it."

"With just one, plant-wide overhead rate?"

"Correct."

"Then let me suggest a few things to keep in mind as you embark on this task. First, indirect manufacturing costs do not all follow direct labor. Some do, but many of them follow the operation of the equipment. Second, you sell a line of products to an industry based on a price list that you then discount to customers, most likely based on sales volume; you do not quote unique products to specific customers. Third, there's an important concept called 'long-term sustainable economics' that you need to keep in mind. Finally, and this one was passed along to me years ago by a mathematics professor, there's almost no phenomenon that you can't describe using a two-by-two matrix."

"A two-by-two matrix?"

"That's what he said, and, although it's probably not a universal truth, I've found it to be an extremely valuable concept when it comes to managerial costing."

"I don't think I understand."

"Well, think of the Boston Consulting Group's corporate portfolio management matrix. That's a good example." The Major began to get up from his seat. "I've got to run. I'll look forward to hearing what you've come up with when I see you again in September."

"Can I get in touch with you during the summer if I have any questions?"

"That's not possible," the Major replied. "I won't be reachable until next September's meeting." With that, the Major finished his Manhattan and headed out the door.

Marcella sat by herself for a few minutes. She appreciated the old guy's counsel, but she wished he weren't so mysterious. *I understand the thing about separating direct labor and indirect manufacturing costs,* she thought to herself, *but I'm not too sure what the other three things have to do with costing our products.* A few moments later, she packed up and began the trip home.

Chapter 15

"What did the Major think?" were the first words out of Alex's mouth as he walked into Marcella's office the next Monday morning. "Did he like the model you and Rich came up with?"

"Yes, he liked it. But more important, how was your golf game this weekend?" Marcella was obviously getting more comfortable with Alex's managerial style and was learning how to play along with his collegial way of dealing with his staff.

"I played well, but not as well as Papasifakis. I had to buy our lunch again. And it was hot, hotter than ..." he paused a moment, "well, hotter than you know where. We should have ridden carts, but as an ex-caddy, I don't like to keep those hard-working kids from earning a few bucks. I remember how ticked off I used to get when the old geezers would walk right past us in the caddy shack on hot days, grab a cart, and ride around the course like they owned the place.

"But let's get back to your distribution model," he continued. "What did the Major say?"

"He paid very close attention while I described our model to him, and he didn't say much until I had finished. He then called me 'Isaac Newton' and congratulated me for inventing my own calculus for the distribution problem. He was surprised that I wasn't heading up the implementation, but he understood when I described the competitiveness issue with small products that you wanted me to address."

"Did he give you any guidance on that problem?"

"I think so."

"You think so? What does that mean?"

"He gave me four bits of advice, but I really understood only one of them. The other three were typical of the mysterious way he alludes to something but doesn't explain it. But I have learned over the past few months that he likes to put the germ of an idea in my head and see if I can figure out what it means as I attack the problem. I hope I'll be able to see how they relate to the problem at hand."

"Well," asked Alex, "what were those four things?"

"First," replied Marcella, "he said that indirect manufacturing costs don't all follow direct labor. Second, that we sell a line of products to an industry based on a price list that we then discount to customers, we do not quote unique products to specific customers. Third, he said that there's an important concept called 'long-term sustainable economics' that we need to keep in mind. And finally, he suggested that there's almost no phenomenon that we can't describe using a two-by-two matrix."

"And which one do you understand?"

"I get the bit about indirect costs not following labor. I've read some about the causality principle and linking costs to their causes using a method like activity-based costing. Do you get anything from the other three?"

Alex thought for a few moments before he answered. "Items two and three sound like warnings to me," he said. "They seem to be warning you to not jump at the obvious answers. It's like he's saying that you'll probably think about costing products like a company that quotes each product individually, but don't do it. The 'long-term sustainable economics' comment seems to imply that the model you come up with needs to consider more than just what happened last year or are anticipating next year. It needs to encompass whatever cost-related insights the company needs in order to prosper for years to come.

"The last item seems more like his discussion of the pet-boarding business a few months back. It's a clue to put you on the trail of a computational method he feels might be appropriate."

"You're probably right," said Marcella, "but I sure wish he would be more direct."

"It's pretty obvious that he wants you and our operating folks to work it out on your own. If he gave you a paint-by-the-numbers answer, you most likely wouldn't fully understand the model, and it might not actually fit the business. It's also pretty clear that he feels confident that you're capable of doing this. I do, too."

"I wish I were as confident as you guys."

The two then went on to discuss a variety of other company issues before the Monday morning session ended and Alex retired to his office.

Chapter 16

Christian Scheele was fairly new as PlumbCo's director of manufacturing. He joined PlumbCo two years prior after a decade working in the industry with several other companies that produced rubber products. Marcella had already worked with him on several projects—none of which, however, required her to take a deep dive into the details of manufacturing the company's products. He was a degreed manufacturing engineer who was passionate about manufacturing and active in the local Society of Manufacturing Engineering chapter and had even had a couple of papers published. Unlike some engineers with whom Marcella had worked, he was also one of the most outgoing and gregarious people she had ever met.

"Hey, Chris!" shouted Marcella as she saw him pass her office.

"Yes, ma'am. You called?" he replied as he backtracked to her door.

"Got a minute?"

"For you, I've got five minutes," he replied as he flopped down in the chair reserved for Alex on Monday mornings. "What's up?"

"Alex has asked me to take a look at the way we cost our products. It's got something to do with marketing's concern that we're more competitive on our larger parts than on our smaller ones. He believes that we do an excellent job at producing both of them, so the problem might lie in the way we determine their costs."

"Or the fact that marketing doesn't know what they're talking about?" Chris replied with a smile.

"I'm not going to touch that one," laughed Marcella. "The fact is he wants me to dive into the costing issue and see if there's an issue there."

"Understood. Sort of like you were doing with Rich in warehousing for the last couple of months, eh? How can I help?"

"The first thing is for me to gain a better understanding of our manufacturing processes. I can talk with outsiders and use the right buzzwords to give the impression I know what I'm talking about, but I'm pretty weak when it comes to the details. I'll need you to give me an education."

"It would be a pleasure. When would you like to embark on this educational experience?"

"We'll probably need a couple of hours to get started. I can't absorb things for much longer than that at one sitting. When would you have that kind of time?"

"For you, I'll make time. How about next Monday afternoon, right after lunch? Unless some kind of emergency comes up, I'll have the week's activity lined up by then and should be able to give you my undivided attention."

"Then how about 1:00 on Monday?"

"Monday at 1:00 it is. Your office or mine?"

"Let's make it yours."

"Consider it booked."

Christian was there waiting for Marcella when she arrived at his office. On his desk were a variety of PlumbCo's parts, a plant layout, and a variety of schematics and diagrams.

"You look prepared," said Marcella as she sat down. It was obvious he liked to talk about his work. *It doesn't look like I'll have to pull teeth to get information out of Chris,* she thought as she settled in.

"Where do you want to start?"

"How about an overview of the manufacturing process? You know, pretty high-level. Something to get a feel for the big picture."

"Okay, let's start with this." Chris pulled out a diagram from his papers and set it in front of Marcella. "This pretty much summarizes what we do."

"You are prepared, aren't you?" said Marcella.

"I aim to please." Chris laughed.

"We'll start at the top," Chris began. "We purchase rubber rolls from a couple of suppliers. There are about 10 different formulations of rubber involved and both these suppliers could provide all of them, but we have enough volume that we can still get a good price while protecting ourselves from a problem at either one of them."

"Sounds wise," interjected Marcella.

"Shearing then cuts the rolls into the ribbons we need for the molding process."

"There's just one shearing machine?"

"Yup, just one. With two operators. We could probably get by with just one, but we've found that we can get the most out of the one machine when we minimize the loading, unloading, and cleaning time by using two operators. They're able to keep

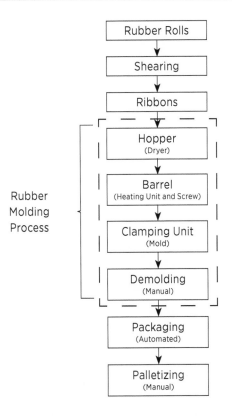

its uptime around 10% higher than one operator and make the likelihood of having to add a third shift minimal."

"So it runs two shifts most of the time?"

"We've been running steady at two shifts for a couple of years now. Once the rubber is in ribbons, it's ready for the molding process.

"You can break the molding process into four steps." He pointed at the diagram. "In the first step, the ribbons required to cover the shot quantity are loaded into the hopper. The shot quantity represents the amount of material needed to completely fill the mold. The hopper includes a dryer that makes sure there's no excess moisture in the material before it enters the second step, which is the barrel. The barrel has both a barrel heater and a screw. The screw forces the material into the barrel where the heater heats the rubber—I bet that was a great revelation to you—to the appropriate viscosity."

"Viscosity?" asked Marcella.

"Viscosity measures the resistance of the rubber to a change in its shape. It's got to be just the right viscosity to flow through the sprue and runners into the mold cavity."

"Whoa, now! I understand mold cavity, but what is a 'sprue' and a 'runner'?"

Chris laughed. "A sprue is a channel through which the rubber enters the mold. A runner is a channel through which the rubber travels from the sprue to the mold's cavities. We also use the terms sprue and runners to describe the residual rubber that remains in the sprue and runners after the molding cycle is completed."

"Okay, I got it now."

"The rubber then flows into the mold, which is held in a clamping unit. It's the clamping unit that applies pressure and is used to define the equipment's 'tonnage' or pressure applied during the molding process. When people talk about a molding 'press,' they are usually speaking about the barrel/clamping unit combination."

"How many operators are needed?"

"Only one operator is needed, but sometimes we find it's better to use two."

"Why would you need two?"

"Because of the fourth step: demolding. Sometimes the time required by the operator to perform all of the demolding steps is longer than the cycle time for the molding of the parts themselves. After the parts are molded, the operator must remove them from the press, clean out any residual rubber sticking to the mold, start the next molding cycle, and separate the parts from their sprues and runners. For some parts, especially when many smaller parts are produced in one mold, the time it takes to separate all of the parts from the sprues and runners takes longer than the mold cycle itself. To keep the flow going and optimize the usage of the molding equipment, we'll add a second person to help the demolding process keep up with the molding process."

"Does it always require that person be there full time? What if you need only a half-person's help?"

"Well, we tried to hire half-persons, but we couldn't find any. Actually, we try to schedule production so that we can share that one additional person between two presses. If we have two parts running that both have the demold time vs. mold time cycle problem, we'll try to run them in proximity to each other and have someone divide their time between the two. However, that is only possible about half the time. The other half of the time we have two people attending a press during the process."

"That doesn't seem very efficient."

"Not from a labor perspective, but from an equipment usage and capacity perspective, it helps us make optimal use of our investment."

"Okay. The parts are separated from the sprues and runners, and then what happens?"

"They're sent to packaging. We have three rotary heat sealers with two workstations each, and the parts are blister-packed at these stations. The operators put the packaged parts in boxes that they stack on pallets. Those pallets are then moved to the warehouse where they come under Rich's domain. That about sums up the high-level view of manufacturing."

"We spend a lot of money on molds, don't we?"

"That's true. Quality molds are critical to the process. We spend a lot of time designing the mold for each new product to make sure it not only makes a quality part, but lasts forever."

"Forever?"

"Well, not really forever. But for many, many years. We seldom have to replace a mold once it's put in service. However, we do pay a lot of attention to maintaining the condition of the molds. After each use, it is cleaned and inspected by our mold-maintenance group. If any maintenance or repair is required, it is done before the mold is put back in storage. The molds we buy are mostly for new parts or are new molds for manufacturing current parts differently."

"How much does a new mold cost?"

"Oh, they can range from $2,000 to $20,000. They probably average about $12,000."

"And how long does it take to set up a press before you start on a new part?"

"The equipment is usually down for 60 to 90 minutes while a couple of our set-up people clean the equipment, get the new mold installed, and make sure a good part is manufactured."

"So there's a separate group of set-up people?"

"Yes, there are five on each shift. We probably need only four, but we're so focused on keeping the equipment running, we keep a fifth on hand as insurance."

Marcella thought for a few moments then asked, "How many presses do we have?"

"We have 12, ranging from 30 tons to 200 tons."

"I would imagine the larger presses cost more to run than the smaller ones."

"Not as much as you might think. The big difference would be electricity. The larger presses make larger parts, meaning they have to heat up more rubber in the barrel before molding. They'd also require more electricity to accommodate the higher tonnage. Their original cost would be higher, of course, but most of the other day-to-day operating costs would be about the same."

Chris then went on to show Marcella where each piece of equipment was located on the plant layout and described the material flows through the plant.

"I think I've hit my limit for one sitting," Marcella said as Chris finished explanations. "But I'll be back for more after I've digested all of this."

"You're welcome out here in the plant anytime," he replied. "I figure the more you know about what we do out here, the better off we all are."

On her way back to her office, Marcella's mind was already working on ways to create a model that reflected all she had learned. She was also trying to figure out how the Major's comments fit in. She could see how the first item, the one about labor and indirect costs, would apply, but she was confused about the others. She was confident the Major's observations were relevant and important; the old guy had proven it with warehousing, but she couldn't quite see how.

Chapter 17

Monday morning found Alex sitting across the desk from Marcella.

"I hear you spent some time with Chris last week," he said after finishing their discussion of the weekend's adventures.

"Yeah, he was very helpful."

"When I talked with him on Friday, he said you were a lot more interested in the details of manufacturing than any other controller he had worked with. He seemed to have enjoyed your interview."

"He certainly was prepared, and he never even implied that any of my questions were dumb." They both laughed. "He seemed to know just how much detail to give me without making it overwhelming."

"That sounds like Chris. Although he likes to make digs at the other folks around here, you can always tell they're good-natured. He's a team player and wants to do what's best for PlumbCo. So what did you get out of your interview?"

"Do you remember the first item the Major mentioned when I last spoke to him? The one about indirect manufacturing costs not always following direct labor?"

"Yes, I remember that one."

"Well, I think that's the big part of our problem."

"How's that?"

"We have a plant-wide overhead rate that follows direct labor. We take the direct labor cost and then add a percentage to that labor cost to assign the indirect manufacturing cost or overhead. But sometimes we have more than one person attending a machine. When that happens, we're not only adding the additional labor to the cost being assigned to the part, we're doubling up on the overhead even though a lot of that indirect cost is related to the equipment, not to the worker. There's still only one press operating, so we're not really incurring all that much more indirect cost. And," she paused for a moment, "most of the time that we need more than one worker is when we're making smaller parts."

"So we're over-costing those parts," interjected Alex.

"That's right: We're doubling the manufacturing cost per hour when maybe it should only be 20% to 30% higher."

"So the marketing folks weren't wrong ... We're most likely over-pricing those parts."

"Most likely," replied Marcella, "but that's not the only issue. The type of equipment, and in the case of molding, the size of the equipment may be a factor."

"How's that?"

"We use the same rate for shearing and packaging that we do for molding. Even with my limited knowledge of manufacturing, it seems pretty clear that operating the shear or blister-packing equipment doesn't cost as much as running the molding presses. And not all of the molding presses cost the same. Larger equipment consumes more electricity. I don't know how much more, but it might make a difference."

"So how do we fix it?" asked Alex.

"Since the crew size can vary when the same press makes different parts, I'm thinking we should separate the indirect costs between those that relate to the worker and those that relate to the equipment, and then apply them separately. The labor-related costs can still be a percentage of the labor, or maybe an additional cost-per-labor hour, but the equipment cost should probably be a cost-per-equipment hour. Also, we should probably have different per-hour costs for different types of equipment."

"That makes sense. Will the cost accounting software handle that?"

"Don't know. I'll have to check into it."

"What if it doesn't?"

"Good question. I haven't thought that far." Marcella hesitated for a moment then added, "But regardless, I don't think we'd want to keep using the bad information. We'll need to figure out something."

"I agree," said Alex, "we certainly don't want to continue to base our pricing on faulty cost information. Were there any other issues that came up during your chat with Chris?"

"Yeah, there were two others that occurred to me, but I don't have any answers for them yet."

"And they were ...?"

"One had to do with set-ups and the other with molds. Set-ups take between an hour and an hour and a half and are performed by people other than the operators. A part with a long set-up but a short production run would result in a high set-up cost per part. On the other hand, a part with a short set-up and a long production run would result in a low set-up cost per part. Depending on the materiality of our set-up costs, that could have a significant impact on the part cost."

"That's true. Couldn't we just incorporate set-ups into the current system?"

"That could be a problem. We have a standard-cost system, not a job-cost system. We can't change the set-up time and the run quantity every time we produce a part to arrive at that run's set-up cost per part. And I'm not too sure we could incorporate a set-up cost at all. That's something else I'll have to check into."

"And the issue with molds?"

"The molds are, obviously, part of the set-up, but they also have what you might call 'a maintenance cycle' that they go through each time they are used. The maintenance cycle isn't performed by the same people who do the set-ups, and the time required doesn't necessarily reflect the time required by the set-up. The maintenance cycle for a particular mold might be a half hour, but the set-up an hour and a half. Or the maintenance cycle two hours and the set-up one hour. Depending on the condition of the mold after it is used, the same mold might require a half hour to maintain one time and two hours the next time. And we still have the problem with a standard-cost system. We can't change the numbers every time we run a part."

"I see what you mean. Maybe we weren't meant to have a standard-cost system."

"I don't know," replied Marcella, "it seems like the most appropriate type of system to me, but I am beginning to wonder."

"How's Jim making out on implementing your ideas about distribution?"

"He's still looking into what it'll take, IT-wise, to make it work. He believes the data is all there, it's a matter of IT being able to pull it together in a way we can use it."

"Well, keep me posted on his progress." Alex looked at his watch. "I've got to run," he said. "Keep up the good work. I like what you've done so far."

Marcella sighed. She was glad the boss was happy with her work, but she wasn't too sure where she was headed next.

Chapter 18

Alex and Theron Papasifakis headed to the club lounge after Alex lost another wager during their just-completed round of golf. After they ordered their drinks and had discussed the problems with Alex's swing, the conversation turned to business.

"How are you coming with your costing issues back at PlumbCo?" asked Theron.

"We're making pretty good progress. I think my controller has come up with some pretty good ideas, both for distribution and manufacturing, but we've still got a way to go."

"Well, fill me in."

Alex proceeded to describe the progress made thus far. "So we're now working on the issues of set-up and mold maintenance," he concluded.

"Interesting," said Theron. "Your controller seems to have come a long way since we first talked."

"Marcella is very sharp. I think she just needed a little nudge to get out of her 'accountant's mindset.' She's also quite good at dealing with her peers. She listens well and doesn't rush to judgment quickly. I think the staff finds it refreshing that she's become interested in the details of what they do. She's becoming a real problem-solving contributor and not just someone who says 'those are the rules and that's how we have to do it.'"

"You're fortunate. In my experience, she seems like the exception, not the rule. Now about these problems with set-ups and molds: Do you have any ideas?"

"Me? Ideas about accounting?" Alex looked astonished that Theron would even ask such a question. They both laughed.

"This Marcella showed a lot of imagination in solving the problems of accounting for distribution," Theron said. "Maybe she should apply some of those same ideas to set-ups and molds."

"How's that?"

"When she was venturing into distribution—an area of costing in which she had no previous experience—she entered without any pre-existing ideas or models. She was going in cold. She had to invent something from scratch. Now, from my experience, the conventional, standard-issue accountant would have tried to create a model that would come up with the exact cost of picking a particular order, the storage cost for each individual part, or the exact cost of processing a specific shipment. But she didn't do that. Whether she did it consciously or not, she took a step back and appears to have asked herself, *What is it that we're trying to learn from this information?*"

"I do recall her making some comments along those lines," interjected Alex.

Theron continued, "Obviously, you were trying to measure how much fulfillment costs eat into the gross margin you earn on each customer's sales so you could understand each customer's true profitability. You were not trying to understand the profitability of each individual order or shipment. You don't quote each order individually, so you don't need the information for quoting. You fill multiple orders for your customers over extended periods of time. What you need to know is how fulfillment costs relate to each customer 'over time.'

"That phrase 'over time' was critical. I believe that was what led her to divide the work of distribution into its key elements and then determine whether the effort for each of those key elements was the same for each product or customer or whether some definable feature made them different. For those where it was different—like orders, line items, and shipments—she came up with a rather ingenious way to account for those differences 'over time.'"

"You're probably right. I don't know exactly how her thought process went, but that does coincide with some of the comments she made during our conversations."

"Now we come to manufacturing. For manufacturing, the situation is different. Where there weren't any ideas and models she could access for distribution, accountants do have ideas and models to account for manufacturing. Accounting texts and literature are filled with them. For some reason, most companies use the easiest and least accurate one, which applies overhead as a percentage of direct labor. That's what you've been doing. Your controller seems to have dug a little deeper into the alternatives and come up with a pretty sound model for handling the bulk of your manufacturing costs. Just adopting that model will undoubtedly improve your product costing tremendously."

"That's good to hear from you," Alex interrupted. "Her model sounded pretty good to me."

"But," Theron went on, "you've still got the issues of set-ups and mold cycles."

"That we do," said Alex, while ordering another drink for himself and his friend.

"Now I imagine that direct labor and indirect manufacturing costs represents about 80%-90% of your total manufacturing costs. Set-up and mold cycle costs probably represent the balance. For purposes of this conversation, let's say it's 85%. That means you're now doing a pretty comprehensive job on 85% of your manufacturing costs. The model being used to assign them to products does reflect the actual operation of your production facility and will result in an acceptable level of accuracy. The appropriate assignment of the other 15% of costs could make a difference in your understanding of product cost, but the question is 'How accurate do they need to be to still wind up with an acceptable level of accuracy for the product's total manufacturing cost?'

"The obvious way is to track the hours and other costs required to do each set-up and execute each mold cycle. If you were quoting each product individually, that's probably the way you'd want to do it. But you don't do that. That level of accuracy probably isn't required. But you do want to take the differences into account. Does that sound familiar?"

Alex thought for a moment. "It sounds like the issue we had with distribution."

"Bingo!" cried Theron. "I think she needs to think like she did with distribution and come up with a simple way to attach set-up and mold cycle costs to products the same way she did distribution costs."

"I'll pass your suggestion along to her. By the way, what are you and your bride up to tonight? Rachel and I are having dinner at Horatio's, want to join us?"

With that, the two friends went on to discuss other matters and plan their evening together.

Chapter 19

It was on a Monday morning three weeks later that Alex found himself sitting across from Marcella again. Vacations had resulted in one or both of them being out of the office for most of the month.

"How was your time off?" asked Marcella.

"Rachel and I had a great time. One of my old Navy buddies has a place in northern Michigan, in the state's ring finger, and he invited us to spend a couple of weeks with him. We found a lot of great places to play golf, got in a bit of fishing, and found some great out-of-the-way places for dinner."

"Where is Michigan's 'ring finger'?" asked Marcella, having never heard this term.

"If you look at a map of Michigan, we were just about where the tip of the ring finger would be inside the mitten."

Marcella laughed.

"Before I forget," continued Alex, "I had a conversation with Theron about our quest for improved costing before I headed out on vacation."

My vacation's over, thought Marcella. *Back to work.* "And what did that great fan of accountants have to say about our quest?" she asked.

Alex smiled. "It's nothing personal," he said, "it's just a reflection of the frustration he's had with accountants over the years." He then proceeded to give Marcella a summary of the exchange he and Theron had three weeks earlier.

"So he thinks we're on the right track?" she asked.

"That he does. He really seemed to like the approach you took for distribution. What do you think about the comments he made about set-ups and mold cycles?"

"I see what he's getting at. It brings to mind something that the Major talked about during one of our conversations. The point he made was that a 10% error in assigning 15% of your cost would only result in a 1.5% error. If you believe you have a great deal of accuracy in assigning the other 85% of the cost, the method you use to assign the other 15% may not need to be all that complex. You just need to heed Oxenfeldt's Rule and find a way to approximate the impact of the major issues related to that other 15%."

"So how do we do it?" asked Alex.

"Beats me," replied Marcella. "At least for now. I'll get with Chris again this week and see if we can't figure something out."

"Sounds like a plan. Speaking of Chris, I've got to catch up with him and see what adventures he had while I was away. Let me know what you and he come up with."

So ended Alex's visit on this Monday morning.

Chapter 20

"Hey Chris!" said Marcella as she stood in Chris Scheele's office doorway. "Am I too early?"

"Yes, you are," he replied, "three whole minutes early. But for you, I'm willing to make a major adjustment in my schedule." They both laughed. "What's on the agenda for today?"

"First, I want to give you my ideas for costing the actual manufacturing processes and then we need to discuss set-ups and mold cycles."

"Okay, shoot!"

Marcella described her idea about separating labor costs from indirect manufacturing costs and assigning them separately—one as a cost-per-labor hour and the other as a cost-per-machine (or equipment) hour—and the reasoning behind her proposal. She then explained how she thought they'd need separate rates for shearing and packing and possibly have multiple rates for molding, depending on the size of the press.

"Those sound like good ideas to me," said Chris. "It's obvious that our shearing and packaging equipment costs a lot less to operate than the molding presses. And it's also pretty obvious that equipment costs aren't double when we have two workers running a piece of equipment instead of only one. The method

you propose would take are of those issues. How many different categories of molding presses do you suggest?"

"I don't know. I believe you said the biggest differences
would relate to original cost and electricity usage. What do
you think?"

"Well," he thought for a moment, "at least two. It's pretty
clear the 30-ton press would be less costly to operate than the
200-ton press, but I'm not sure where the cutoff between the
two categories would be. Maybe we'd need a third category in
the middle."

"I'll tell you what," said Marcella, "let's make a list of the 12
presses. I'll look up their original cost and annual depreciation
in our property records, and you look up their annual uptime
and come up with an estimate of each press' electricity usage.
I believe I can give you a total electricity cost for the press room;
you'll just have to break it down."

"Do you want an educated guess? Or do I need to check
horsepower on the motors and do some calculations?"

"An educated guess is good enough for now."

"No problem!"

"We can table any decision about press categories until we
see what the numbers look like once we put them all together."

"Sounds like a wise thing to do."

"But now we come to our set-ups and mold cycles."

"So what's so tough about them?" asked Chris.

"We already have routings for all of our parts and they
include shearing, molding, and packaging as steps in the production process. Although it will take some time and effort to
modify those routings to reflect the multiple indirect cost rates
and to separate the labor costs, I believe our system will be able

to handle those changes. Jim's been looking into the software's capabilities to confirm that it's possible. All of those changes relate to the cost per hour of performing each manufacturing process. The number of parts being produced during a production run doesn't matter. Just the cost per hour and the number of parts we can produce in an hour.

"Set-ups and mold cycles, however, occur once each production run. They aren't a cost per hour, they're a cost per production run or 'batch.' Their impact on the cost per part will depend on the size of the batch being run." Marcella thought about what she said and then asked, "Is the batch size the same every time you run a particular part number?"

"Nope," replied Chris, "it differs from run to run, depending on the anticipated demand for that part."

"Sometimes it can be a long run and at other times a short run?"

"Not really. A popular part's run can range from long to longer to longest, and a less-popular part's run can range from short to shorter to shortest. I don't recall ever having a part having both long and short runs. Each part's run is always within some segment of the spectrum of run sizes, but a part in the red segment of the spectrum never has one in the violet segment."

"Spectrum? Red segment? Violet segment? What are you talking about?"

"Don't you remember Roy G. Biv?" asked Chris. "Didn't you pay attention in science class?"

"Oh! Okay. I get it." Marcella smiled. "There's a range of lengths in production runs just like there are ranges of colors in the visible-light spectrum. If red is a short run and violet is a long run, each part will always be somewhere within its color—a short run will always be in the red—but it won't necessarily be in the exact same place. Is that what you're saying?"

"That's what I'm saying."

"You sometimes have a strange way of expressing your ideas."

"I like to be colorful, if you'll pardon the pun."

They both laughed. It was clear that Chris was a different sort of character.

"Accounting-wise, the most appropriate way to handle both set-ups and mold cycles—I'll refer to them as events—would be to measure the cost of the event and divide it by the number of parts produced in the production run. That's probably how we'd want to do it if we were quoting a specific part for a specific customer. It could have a significant impact on the cost of that one part."

Marcella hesitated and remembered her last conversation with the Major. Almost hearing him whispering in her ear, she added, "But we sell a line of products to an industry based on a price list that we may discount to certain customers. We do not quote unique products to specific customers."

"And what is the significance of that?" interjected Chris.

"It's not an individual product's profitability that we're concerned about; it's the profitability of lines or categories of products. We wouldn't drop a couple of unprofitable products if they were necessary to keep a line of products intact. It's that line or family of products we sell. We wouldn't be a viable supplier if we didn't carry the whole line." She looked at Chris. "Sorry, I'm thinking out loud. You're listening to my brain try to work."

"No, go on," said Chris, "I'm fascinated."

"If we were to have a family of all short runners with difficult set-ups, which thankfully I don't believe we do, we'd want to make sure the parts in that family were assigned a pretty high set-up cost. On the other hand, if we had a family of long runners with easy set-ups, we'd want to make sure those have a low set-up cost per part. If another family were half one and half the other, we'd want the set-up cost per part to be somewhere in the middle. The same holds true for mold cycles. We want the family or category to reflect the level of mold cycle cost that its parts require, but knowing the exact cost per part isn't necessary."

Chris sat there, smiling. "Keep going," he said. "How are we going to accomplish this without doing the whole 'accounting-wise' thing you described earlier?"

"The matrix! That's where that damn matrix comes in!" Marcella surprised herself with her little outburst. "The two-by-two matrix!"

"Okay, I was with you until then. Are you trying to get even with me for talking about spectra?"

"No. A few months ago, a wise old friend of mine planted the idea in my head that there's almost no phenomenon that you can't describe using a two-by-two matrix. Let me try this on you.

"The impact of both set-ups and mold cycles on parts cost is the result two factors: the cost of the event and the number of parts that follow the event." She pulled out a piece of paper and started scribbling. After a few moments, she slid it in front of Chris and said, "Look at this."

Production Run

		Short	Long
Event Cost	High	High Cost/ Short Run	High Cost/ Long Run
	Low	Low Cost/ Short Run	Low Cost/ Long Run

"Two factors determine the cost per part: the cost of the event and the number of parts in the production run. Dividing both factors into two categories that represent their opposite halves, we have event costs that can be high or low and production runs that can be long or short. Using these four categories, we could create a two-by-two matrix and assign each part to the quartile that describes it best. We could then use the 'weighting' process to come up with a cost per part in each quartile of the matrix and include that cost in the standard we establish in our system."

"I'm a little less lost, but still lost nevertheless," was Chris' reaction. "And what the heck is 'the weighting process'?"

"I forgot. You don't know about that. We used it in distribution. Give me a minute or two to put together an example."

Chris checked the messages on his cell phone while Marcella worked on her example.

"Okay," she finally said, "see if you can follow this."

Cost/Run	Parts	Weight	Weighted Parts	Pct	Dollars	Cost per Part
Low/Long	750,000	1.0	750,000	17.0%	$170,455	$0.23
Low/Short	300,000	2.0	600,000	13.6%	$136,364	$0.45
High/Long	750,000	3.0	2,250,000	51.1%	$511,365	$0.68
High/Short	200,000	4.0	800,000	18.2%	$181,818	$0.91
Totals	2,000,000		4,400,000	100.0%	$1,000,000	

"Assume we produce two million parts and the total cost of the set-ups or mold cycles is $1,000,000." She looked Chris in the eye. "Remember, the numbers are made up for the example. No cracks like 'does it really cost $1,000,000 to do set-ups?'"

"I take it you've run into problems explaining your examples before?"

"Yes, I have, so no cracks."

"Understood."

"Okay. Now, intuition tells us that the low-event-cost/long-part-run parts will be the least costly, so we'll give them a weight of 1.0. Intuition also tells us that the most costly parts will be those with high-event-cost/short-part-runs. The question then becomes 'How much more costly, relative to the low-cost/long-run parts, will the event cost be for the high-cost/short-run parts?' Since we're talking 'relative' here, the answer should be a multiple of the weight assigned to the low/long parts. In this case, I gave it a 4.0. We expect the unit cost to be four times higher. You with me so far?"

"With you so far."

"We then assign weights reflecting the cost of the other two categories relative to the low/long parts. Of course, they will be somewhere between the two extremes that we've already defined: 1.0 and 4.0. In my example, I gave the low/short category a 2.0 and the high/long category a 3.0. We then do some math."

"I can do the math," interrupted Chris. "After all, I'm an engineer and I think I can see where you're going." He then proceeded to describe—quite accurately—the rest of the calculations required to arrive at the event cost per part.

"You've done this before?" asked Marcella.

"No. It's the first time I've seen a finance guy—excuse me, finance person—look at things this way. Once you started, however, the balance of your logic seemed pretty clear. This would get us four average unit costs for both set-ups and mold cycles. We could identify which categories each part belongs in and then assign that cost per unit to each part in our standard-cost system. One unit cost for set-up and another for mold cycle. *N'est-ce pas?*"

"*Exactement!*" exclaimed Marcella. "*Trou en un!*"

"Let's get back to English. The only French I know is *n'est-ce pas* and *s'il vous plait*. I think I understood '*exactement*,' but what does '*trou en un*' mean?"

"It means you got a 'hole in one.'"

"Great! I've never had one of those before." Chris laughed. "But I've still got a question."

"Shoot!"

"I understand how we can have someone go through the parts and assign each one to a category. It'll be time consuming, but it won't be difficult. I can also understand how you'll be able to come up with the total cost of performing the set-ups and mold changes. What I don't understand is how we're going to come up with the weights. Who's going to do it? And how are they going to do it?"

"I hadn't given that much thought yet," answered Marcella, "but let's talk about it. Keep in mind that we're not trying to be exact here, just reasonably accurate. We're using Oxenfeldt's Rule here."

"Oxenfeldt's Rule?" inquired Chris.

"I guess I haven't mentioned that to you, have I?" She then gave him a brief description of that concept.

"Okay, I'm with you. Continue on, oh venerable sage."

"The easiest way would be to get the folks who perform these activities in a room, walk them through the thought process, and have them come up with their best estimates. If we don't want to rely on just their experience, we could select a few parts from each category and use our historical data to measure their average event cost per unit during the past six months or year. We could then use those measures to arrive at the weights."

"That should work," said Chris. "I've got one more question: How about the cost of the molds themselves? Each part has a mold that's used exclusively for that part. Right now, I think you amortize the molds over three or four years and include the amortization cost in overhead."

"Another good question. That is how we do it, but now that I'm getting deeper into this costing stuff, I'm not too sure it's the right way to account for it. It certainly doesn't link mold costs with individual parts very well. Molds last a lot more than three or four years, so the molds for a lot of our parts are fully amortized and would result in zero mold cost for those parts. Others are newer, but the amortization period is much shorter than the mold's life, so those parts would be getting an excessive mold charge until, suddenly, when the three- or four-year amortization periods ends, they would be getting none. But then again, do we need to link it to individual parts? I'm going to have to think about this a bit more."

"Is there anything I need to do in the meantime?" asked Chris.

"No, not right now. We need to bounce this idea off Alex and the IT folks. We need to make sure the boss is comfortable with what we've come up with as well as ensure that the software will handle these extra 'per-part' costs we'd come up with. I'll probably ask you to join the discussion when I talk to Alex about this."

"You say the word, and I'll be there. Anything else?"

"No, I think we're done for the day. Thanks for all your help."

"No problem, *mon amie!*"

"I thought you didn't know any more French," replied Marcella.

"I lied," answered Chris.

Chapter 21

"Am I interrupting something?" asked Jim Stinson as he stood outside of Marcella's office.

"No, come on in," she replied. "What's up?"

"I thought I'd update you on my discussions about distribution with Rich and the IT folks."

Marcella had been so focused on the costing issues in manufacturing that she hadn't thought about implementing the changes for distribution for several weeks. She was glad that Jim was one of those employees who didn't need a lot of supervision. In his short time with PlumbCo, he had already proven to be someone who would "grab the ball and run" with any assignment he was given.

"What have you learned?" she asked.

"Since customers in the three customer groups are already tagged in the system, there's no problem in sorting the units and line items by customer. We can get good counts on them."

"That's promising."

"The other items—orders and shipments—do present IT with a problem. They can separate electronic orders from the other orders, but there's nothing in the system to separate the telephone orders from the mail and fax orders. They're both entered manually, but that's all the system knows. However, Rich indicated that he could separate the manually entered orders into the two categories because most customers are pretty consistent in placing their orders one way or the other.

"As for shipments, the system has the information to separate the boxes and pallets as well as count the returns. However, the IT folks aren't sure whether they'd be able to split the loose-part boxes from the single-part boxes."

Marcella looked doubtful. "It would seem like they should be able to see when multiple part numbers are included in the box shipment and when only one part number is included."

"That's what I thought as well," said Jim, "so I asked if they could write a program to do just that. Take all the box shipments and separate them between those containing a single part number and those containing multiple part numbers."

"And they said?"

"They'd look into it. You know how they are," said Jim with a smile, "always backed up with requests and having to put your request into the queue."

"Well, if they don't think they can get to it soon, let me know and I'll see if Alex can encourage them to move it up a bit. He's anxious to get some answers on customer profitability."

"Will do. There is a bigger problem, however."

"Of course."

"Pulling all this data out of the system is one thing, but the software doesn't provide for assigning the costs to customers. They checked, and the software provider doesn't have an add-on module that will do it either. They said they'd either need to have one written—we don't have the in-house capability to do it ourselves—or purchase some kind of add-on software."

"Are they looking for some such software?"

"I don't think so. They probably need some additional motivation."

"I'll try to see that they get it."

"One more thing," said Jim. "I figured we're going to need to come up with the cost for performing each of these five different distribution activities, so I started building an Excel model that would enable us to do so in some logical manner."

This guy certainly knows how to make himself a valuable employee, thought Marcella.

Jim continued, "I read up a bit on causality-based costing and how you can use causality to 'cascade' the company's expenditures through its key activities to its cost objects, and I'm taking that approach to structure the model."

"Great," said Marcella. She thought a moment and then added, "Keep in mind that we're going to need to add manufacturing activities to your model as well. Chris and I are working on the details of how we're going to configure that right now."

"Okay, I'll keep that in mind."

"Anything else to report?"

"No. That's about it for now."

"Well, great job. Keep me posted."

Chapter 22

"I've got something to show you," said Alex as he sat down for his customary Monday morning visit with his controller. "I asked Jim to put a few numbers together for me—I hope you don't mind my asking one of your people to do a quick project for me when you're not around—and here's what he came up with."

"No problem," replied Marcella as she looked at what Alex had handed her. It was a pretty simple summary. "You're the boss. If you need something and I'm tied up elsewhere, you're welcome to go straight to the source."

Customers		% of	% Sales per
No.	%	Sales	Customer
15	1.8%	60.0%	4.000%
85	10.0%	25.0%	0.294%
100	11.8%	85.0%	
750	88.2%	15.0%	0.020%
850	100.0%	100.0%	

"I'm more comfortable going through the chain of command," said Alex, "but I didn't think you'd mind. Anyway," he continued, "I know we don't have numbers for the distribution costs yet, but I was thinking about what they might tell us about our lower-volume customers. So I asked Jim to give me a breakdown of customers by annual sales dollars from highest to lowest. The report itself was 16 pages long, but I think Jim knew what I was after—he is smart, isn't he?—so he added this nice, concise summary.

"Our top 15 customers account for 60% of our annual sales. The top 100 customers account for 85% of our sales. So 85% of our sales were accounted for before the end of page 2! The other 14 pages had only 15%. It's really going to be interesting to find out how much the distribution costs eat into the margins of those 750 customers. This is one place where knowing the difference between a customer who orders 10 of one item and one that orders one each of 10 items will come into play. Or if one of those small customers has a habit of returning items."

"That will be interesting," interjected Marcella. "It'll also be interesting when we get the production costing straightened out to see if the product mix has an impact on the margins themselves. What they buy may have a significant impact as well."

"Speaking of production costing, how'd you make out with Chris?"

"We had a great meeting. He liked the approach I suggested for segregating labor from equipment costs and having different rates for different types of equipment."

"And how about the set-ups and mold cycles?"

"I think we came up with a solution for those, but I'd like to have Chris with us when we go over our proposal."

"So you're not going to tell me about it now?"

"I told Chris I'd invite him to the meeting when we discuss our ideas."

"How about a hint?"

"Okay," laughed Marcella, "but just a hint. We're thinking of using the two-by-two matrix idea to approximate a cost per part for both set-ups and mold cycles."

"A two-by-two matrix, eh? Sounds like something I recall from your last conversation with the Major."

"Yup, that's where the idea came from. I really hadn't much of a clue about what he was talking about until Chris and I got to talking about the set-up and mold cycle issues. That's when it clicked."

"Well, round up Chris and arrange for the three of us to get together as soon as you can. I want to know how this two-by-two matrix will work."

The following day, Marcella and Chris met with Alex to explain their ideas on set-ups and mold cycles. After he got satisfactory answers to all his questions, Alex blessed their approach and gave the order "full speed ahead."

Chapter 23

Marcella hadn't been able to consult with the Major for three months—not since the June IMA meeting—and she was really looking forward to having another opportunity to talk with him about their progress at PlumbCo. She especially wanted to know what he thought of her use of the two-by-two matrix. As the meeting date neared, she put together a short list of items she wanted to make sure she mentioned during their post-meeting chat. At least, she hoped there'd be a post-meeting chat. His appearances were always a bit surreal and she was never sure he was there until he suddenly appeared. Nevertheless, she prepared, assuming he'd make it.

Her list included:

1) separating the labor rate from equipment rates,
2) calculating different rates for shearing, molding, and packing,
3) separating molding into two or three different rates based on the equipment's original cost and electricity consumption,
4) using the two-by-two matrix to measure and assign set-up and mold cycle costs, and
5) the problem of how to account for mold costs.

She wasn't surprised when she didn't see the Major before or during the meeting, but she did begin to get concerned when he was nowhere in sight while she was saying her good-byes to the other attendees. Soon, she was the only member left in the room. Still no Major. Had something happened to him during the summer? Had he just missed the meeting? Maybe, just maybe … she took a look into the lounge. There at one of the tables was an elderly, one-armed, neatly dressed gentleman, sipping on a Manhattan, with a glass of white wine on the other side of his table.

"Mrs. DeCou," he said calmly when he saw her, "I'm so glad to see you. How was your summer?"

"Major!" she exclaimed, "I was afraid you weren't here tonight. I've got a lot to tell you."

"I try to never miss one of these meetings. An old guy like me still needs to keep up on things. Please, have a seat and tell me about your summer."

Marcella wanted to ask him about his summer. As a matter of fact, she wanted to ask him a lot of questions about himself, but it was apparent from their earlier meetings that he didn't want to talk about his history. He just wanted to talk shop with her. She didn't want to risk the relationship they'd built since the beginning of the year, so she kept all of her questions to herself.

"I won't bore you with my family's adventures while on vacation, I'll cut to the quick and bring you up to speed on PlumbCo's adventures in managerial costing."

"I'd love to hear about your family vacation, but I'll settle for your costing adventures."

"By the way," added Marcella, "you don't have to call me Mrs. DeCou. You can call me Marcella."

"You're kind to offer, but I was brought up to call ladies in business 'Miss' or 'Mrs.' And I am inclined to keep that habit. I hope you don't mind."

"No. I don't mind," she answered. *The Major really is old school, isn't he?* she thought to herself. She then went through her list describing her discussions with Chris and Alex and laying out the proposed handling of PlumbCo's manufacturing activities.

"My old friend Alex Church would be happy to see you using machine rates for the equipment," the Major said when she was done. "I don't think, however, that he would have thought to break out the labor rates."

"Alex Church? I don't think I've heard of him."

"Alex was an industrial engineer I once worked with when I was in England. He was a great proponent of machine rates. He also didn't think much of us accountants."

"Sounds like my boss' golfing buddy Theron Papasifakis. He doesn't think much of accountants either."

"I'm afraid they both have good reasons. When it comes to managerial costing, most accountants have been, and are still, too focused on accounting rules and not focused enough on economic reality. But I digress. Explain your logic with regard to using the matrices again."

Marcella went over her rationale for using matrices for set-ups and mold cycles, this time showing the Major the examples she had developed for Chris.

The Major sat silently for a few moments and then said, "You've done very well in incorporating three of the four things I mentioned to you at our last meeting. You've separated the labor costs from the equipment costs. That's particularly important when the crew size attending a machine can vary from product to product. You've also taken into account the objective of your cost information when determining the accuracy required. You must price a wide family of products to the market; you don't quote each part individually. As a result, you can accept a somewhat lower level of accuracy on each individual product, providing it still gives a materially accurate assessment of each product in the family's cost. And you've used the two-by-two matrix concept to ensure that product costs are accurate enough for your purposes. I think you've done an excellent job in crafting a model for the manufacturing processes."

Marcella looked pleased.

"Tell me," continued the Major, "what do you suppose PlumbCo would do if—after using the costs measured using your two-by-two matrices—you found out that low production volumes for 10% of a product line's products make them losers? Would you raise the prices? Would you drop the products? What would you do?"

"That's a good question," answered Marcella. "I've been so focused on developing a model to generate more accurate cost information that I hadn't thought a lot about the results it might generate or the actions we might want to take as a consequence." She paused for a moment. "I don't think raising prices would help. Our prices are pretty much set by the marketplace. Raising prices on 10% of a particular product line might cause a customer to move all of its business somewhere else. Our customers don't buy some products in a product line from one vendor and some from another. They buy a particular line of products from a single vendor.

"I'm also pretty sure we wouldn't drop the losers from the product line because then that line of products would be incomplete. Like raising prices, that might lead a customer to move all of its business to a vendor with a complete product line. I'm pretty sure we'd need to keep the entire product line intact."

The Major took a sip of his Manhattan and grinned. "Then what good does an accurate measure of each product's cost do you? You can't raise prices. You dare not drop products. Is there any action the company can take in response to the insights provided by your improved cost information?"

"It sure doesn't seem so, does it?" Marcella looked perplexed. "All this work to come up with good cost information, and what does it get us?"

"How about customer profitability?" posed the Major. "Could it impact the way you make decisions about customers?"

"Like how?" asked Marcella.

"Well, as I recall you have list prices, but you give different customers different discounts, most likely based on their sales volume. Is my recollection correct?"

"Yes, that's correct."

"What if one of those customers bought a mix of products that included a lot of those low-volume, low-margin parts? Would you want to give them a bigger discount if they bought even more of them? Not enough to turn them into winners instead of losers, but more?"

"Probably not. I guess we could take that mix into account when we determine the discount we'd offer them."

"Along with their ordering behavior. Don't forget how the fulfillment costs eat into the product margin on a customer's purchases."

"You're right. It looks like volume isn't a very good basis for determining discounts, does it?"

"Not volume alone. Measuring customer profitability includes a lot of factors, including product mix and fulfillment requirements. But that's not all you can do with your new understanding of product costs. You can consider building a larger bank of those parts to water down the impact of set-up and mold cycle costs. You can consider outsourcing some of the low-volume parts. You don't want to be myopic and look at the problem from a single perspective. You need to use your imagination."

"I can see that," replied Marcella.

"Let me summarize for a moment. You market product lines to customers. They order what they need of that product line, but you market the line, not individual items. Because the mix of products they order from a product line can have an impact on a customer's profitability—and should have an impact on the discount you allow them—it's important to have a reasonably good handle on the margin generated by each part in the product line so you can understand the profitability of the customer. An extremely accurate measurement would be nice, but it would also be a lot of work, and the climb might not be worth the view. Because of the nature of your business, you do need to take all of the relevant cost factors into account, but a reasonably accurate measure of the less critical factors should be sufficient. Does that sound right to you?"

"Makes perfect sense," answered Marcella. "By the way, you're the second person I've heard use the expression 'is the climb worth the view?' Rich Vivian, the guy who runs our warehouse, also used it."

"It's a good question to ask yourself once you've developed a cost model that effectively handles 80 to 90% of the costs involved and you're deciding how to handle the balance. In your case, the separation of labor and indirect manufacturing costs, the breakdown of the indirect manufacturing costs into rates for different processes, and the further breakdown of molding press rates probably covers that 80 to 90%. As you proceed to model the rest of the costs, you should ask yourself that question for each factor you consider. Are there any consequences if you just bury those costs somewhere else? Is there any benefit to be gained from an accurate assignment of those costs? If so, how accurate do they need to be to gain that benefit?

"That's pretty much what you've done for set-ups and mold cycles. There are consequences if you just bury them. Parts produced in large lots will be subsidizing parts produced in small lots. So will parts with high-cost set-ups or expensive mold cycles. There are benefits to be gained by accurately assigning these costs. You can develop better discounting policies and identify possible cost-reduction opportunities. However, because of materiality, you don't have to model these costs the same, more complex way you would if they were a more substantial part of the total." The Major paused for a moment before adding, "As the song goes, 'two out of three ain't bad,' but what are you going to do about those mold costs?"

He's heard of Meatloaf? Marcella thought to herself.

"Yes, I've heard of Meatloaf," said the Major, reading the expression on her face. "I may be old, but I haven't been unconscious all these years. And I never stop dealing with 'up and coming' younger folks, like you. Now what about mold costs?"

"They do seem to fall into the same category of set-ups and mold cycles: They're not a large percentage of cost, but they're too important to just bury somewhere else."

Just then, Marcella's cell phone rang. "It's my husband," she apologized as she answered the call. "No, I'm all right. I guess the Major and I have run a bit long this evening. Sorry, honey.

I'll be home pretty soon. Okay. Bye." She looked back at the Major. "I guess we've been talking quite awhile this evening."

"Our conversation has been at least two Manhattans and two glasses of wine long," smiled the Major. "Maybe we should wrap it up for tonight."

"Probably so," replied Marcella, a bit disappointed.

"A few points before we call it an evening. You took into consideration only three out of the four items I mentioned when we met last June. Do you recall the other one?"

"The other one?" Marcella paused. "You mean the one about 'long-term sustainable economics'?"

"That's the one. As you consider what to do about mold costs, combine that idea with the fact that your goal is not to be extremely accurate in costing every part, but to be accurate enough to have a good understanding of product and customer profitability."

"Can you explain 'long-term sustainable economics' for me?"

"Sure. In costing, 'long-term sustainable economics' refers to the resources required to maintain the company at its current volume of business over the long run. It's a forward-looking concept. Not what resources did it take to get to where you're at nor what resources will it take to get you where you're going, but what resources will you need to stay where you are."

"I'm not sure I understand."

"Give it some thought. You've proven to me that you've got some pretty good instincts. See what you can come up with before next time."

"Which will be next month?" Marcella wanted some assurance her muse would be there for her.

"God willin' and the creek don't rise," answered the Major as he finished his Manhattan, wished her a good night, and disappeared into the lobby.

Chapter 24

Jim Stinson was in Marcella's office going over the status of implementing the new model for warehousing costs. The IT folks had agreed to write a program to split the loose-part boxes from the single-part boxes, but they hadn't done so yet. They were also in the process of looking for compatible software that could access their files and attach cost to customers. They were moving, but not very fast.

"I'll see if Alex can light a fire under them," said Marcella. "By the way, you've sat in a classroom more recently than I ... Have you ever heard the expression 'long-term sustainable economics' used in connection with costing?"

"Long-term sustainable economics? In connection with costing? Can't say I have. Why do you ask?"

"The Major—he's the elderly gentleman I talk to at my IMA meetings—suggested that long-term sustainable economics was a key to accounting for our mold costs. He says that 'long-term sustainable economics' refers to the resources required to maintain the company at its current volume of business over the long run. To me, it suggests that the numbers reported in our general ledger, those that reflect what has happened recently, are not necessarily the numbers we should use in measuring our costs."

"That does sound familiar. I believe I read something a while back about the danger of using expense information as determined under GAAP in calculating costs. It was something about how accounting's periodicity assumption distorts the underlying nature of a company's expenses as it measures them between arbitrary cutoff dates. It basically said that expenses measured during a month, a quarter, or a year do not necessarily represent the normal level of spending required to support the business. They could be higher than normal during some of those arbitrary periods and lower than normal in others."

"Were there any examples?"

"I do remember one example: It related to research and development." Jim paused for a moment to gather his thoughts. "Let's assume you have a business that's spending $1,000,000 on research and development every year and is growing at 25% per year. The question was, 'Is $1,000,000 required to support the level of business during that period?' Because R&D expense is incurred to support future business, not current business, part of the $1,000,000 could be required to support the current level of business, and part of it is actually an investment made to grow the business. That's probably the case in the example. On the other hand, the 25% growth is the product of R&D expense incurred in earlier periods. The $1,000,000 could be less than required to maintain that growth. In fact, it could be much less than required to support the current level of business."

"Any other examples you can remember?"

"Yes," Jim replied, "now that you ask. Maintenance was another. It talked about equipment that required major maintenance after every 5,000 hours of operating time. However, the equipment ran only 2,000 hours per year. So during some years, it incurred little or no maintenance expenses for the equipment, while in other years, it required all the maintenance needed to keep it operating for another 2 ½ years. The question was, 'Should the maintenance required for 5,000 hours of run time be matched with the 2,000 hours it runs in some years while in other years no maintenance cost is matched against the 2,000 hours?'"

"I see." Marcella was trying to associate Jim's examples with the costing of molds. Suddenly, her expression changed. "The proper amount of expense should be that required to 'sustain' the business at the level being reported or assumed. If the equipment in your example runs 1,600 hours one year and 2,400 hours the next, the second year should have 50% more maintenance in Year 2 than in Year 1—regardless of when the money is actually spent."

"That sounds right," answered Jim. "The maintenance expense relates to—or is driven by—run time, not the time it takes the earth to orbit the sun or the moon to orbit the earth."

"Earth to orbit the sun? Moon to orbit the earth?"

"That's the satirical way the author referred to the arbitrariness of the annual and monthly time periods. He even suggested (with tongue in cheek, I assume) that we adopt the metric accounting year: 1,000 days in the accounting year, 100 days in an accounting month, and 10 days in an accounting week. He argued that it would make the same amount of sense as what we do now."

"I think I get his point. If we want to understand the long-term economics that underlie a business, we can't simply take our general ledger costs and run with them. We've got to understand its 'long-term sustainable economics.'"

"I agree, that's the point that was being made."

"But our molds are investments, not expenses." Marcella was trying to tie this new idea to the Major's comments about mold costs. "They're capitalized and amortized—like capital equipment, only over shorter time periods. Time periods: maybe they're the key. We're getting distortions in mold costs because of the periodicity assumption. I've got to think about this some more. Thanks Jim. You've been a lot of help."

"No problem. That's what I'm here for."

As Jim left her office, Marcella thought, *This guy's a gem. I hope we can hold on to him.*

Chapter 25

Marcella arranged to meet with Chris Scheele a few days later. She found him talking with several of his supervisors when she arrived. The meeting broke up a few minutes later.

"Sorry to keep you waiting, *mon amie*," he said when everyone had departed.

"Not French again," she laughed.

"*Je vous demande pardon*," he replied. "Okay, I'll stick to English. What's on the agenda for today?"

"Mold costs."

"Ah yes, our unfinished business from last time."

"That's right. By the way, have I ever mentioned the Major during one of our conversations?"

"The Major? No, I don't believe so. Who or what is the Major?"

Marcella proceeded to tell Chris about the mysterious, elderly gentleman who had been helping her negotiate through the maze of PlumbCo's costing issues.

"He sounds like a godsend," said Chris after she had finished.

"I sometimes wonder," she replied. "Anyway, the Major seems to think the idea of long-term sustainable economics is important in our approach to mold costs."

"Long-term sustainable economics? You've lost me there."

After providing the best explanation of the concept she could muster, including the examples Jim had used, she asked, "Does it strike any kind of chord with you?"

Chris sat silently for a few moments and then said, "Jim's maintenance example resonates a bit. The maintenance expense is incurred every two or three years, but to truly match maintenance with the operation of the equipment being maintained, we need to make it a function of the hours the machine operates. Ignore when the money is spent. Focus instead on the thing that makes the expense necessary."

"Yes, that seems to be the idea."

"Couldn't we look at buying molds in the same light?"

"How do you mean?"

"Going back to the idea that our focus is on product lines, not on individual products, couldn't we look at the purchase of molds as a necessary cost of maintaining a product line? Whether it's a mold for a new part or a replacement mold, we're spending the money to keep a product line complete. And molds wear out by using them, not by owning them. Chronological time doesn't drive the need to buy molds. Usage drives that need."

"I see your point," replied Marcella, "but molds are capitalized investments, not expenses."

"Does it matter?" asked Chris.

Marcella thought for a few moments. "Maybe it's the accountant in me that's having a problem here. I want to capitalize a long-lived asset and spread it over the future periods it benefits. But obviously, taking a $12,000 mold that will be used for a different number of hours each year for the next 6–8 years and expensing $4,000 per year for 3 years but then nothing for the remainder of its life doesn't really make any sense. If we use it

500 hours the first year, it'll cost $8 per hour. Then if we use it only 250 hours the second year, the cost will be $16 per hour. If we use it 500 hours the fifth year, there will be no cost at all. However, what we do now is just take the $4,000 and stick it in overhead for the first 3 years after we buy the mold. After that, nothing. Ideally, we'd divide the $12,000 by the number of hours the mold will be used during its life, and use that cost per hour every year. But that would be a massive amount of detailed work for a cost that, although it is important, isn't a large percentage of our total costs."

Chris interrupted her train of thought. "But our concern is accurately measuring product line and ultimately customer profitability, not the exactness with which we assign costs to individual parts. We want to make sure parts with a low mold cost are assigned less than those with a high mold cost. We just don't want the way we handle mold costs to distort our understanding of where our profits or losses come from."

"I'm beginning to think you understand this more than I do," said Marcella.

"I'm just not burdened with all your knowledge about accounting," laughed Chris. "I don't care if we violate your accounting rules as long as we get the right answer."

"You're right. I'm still getting hung up on accepted accounting practices. Getting back to your question, 'Does it matter?' With maintenance, we spend money periodically to maintain the equipment. With molds, we spend money periodically to maintain the product line. Does how we bookkeep that money really matter when we think in terms of long-term sustainable economics? Probably not. They're both expenditures to sustain some element of our business over the long term."

"That's the way I'm thinking," interjected Chris.

"So where does that get us?"

The two of them just sat and stared ahead for a few minutes. Finally, Chris asked, "Want a cup of coffee or a water?"

"A bottle of water would be nice," answered Marcella.

"Let's go down the hall and not think about molds for a few minutes."

The two of them walked to the kitchenette, where Marcella grabbed a bottle of water from the small refrigerator and Chris made himself a coffee.

"I liked it better when we kept a fresh pot on the burner in here. The coffee was better, and pouring a coffee is a lot quicker than sticking those little bags in the machine and waiting for it to brew. When they make me emperor, I'll outlaw these single-cup contraptions."

They chatted about a variety of sundry topics until Chris looked at his watch and said, "It's been about 10 minutes. Break time is over. Better get back to work."

Upon arriving back in his office, Chris suggested, "Let's hit the clear button and start from scratch. Try to pretend you don't know any of the accounting rules. I won't need to pretend, so let's start with what we know about molds and then construct a way to assign those costs to products."

"Okay," replied Marcella. "What do we know about molds?"

"Let's start with the cost of a mold. Molds can cost anywhere between $2,000 and $20,000. Using that idea of yours that anything can be explained in a two-by-two matrix, I can identify the two factors that most impact a mold's cost. One factor is the complexity of the mold. Some molds are pretty basic while others have complex internal systems with ejector pins, springs, guide pins, sprue pullers, and all kinds of goodies. Obviously, the more complex one will cost more than the basic one.

"The other factor is the anticipated usage of the mold. If we anticipate heavy usage—meaning we plan on making a whole lot of parts with the mold for a long time—we'll require a higher level of quality than if we believe it will be used for a low volume of parts. No sense buying a Cadillac when you only need a Chevy.

"I could probably come up with a reasonable estimate of the average mold cost in each quadrant of the matrix. It wouldn't be exact, but it would skew that factor in calculating the mold cost per part in the right direction. Are you with me so far?"

"Yes, I'm with you," answered Marcella, a bit startled by the way Chris suddenly seemed to have become so comfortable and confident in explaining costing issues.

"Good. The next question is 'How many parts can we expect this mold to produce?' You said the ideal way to cost would be to take the mold cost and divide by the number of parts it would produce, right?"

"That's what I said," she replied.

"The life of a mold is best measured in the number of cycles it will last, not the amount of time it will be in use. If a mold is expected to last 10,000 cycles and has 6 cavities, its estimated life would be 60,000 parts. It doesn't matter whether those 10,000 cycles occurred over 500 hours, or 1,000 hours, or 3,000 hours; the cost per part would be the same. Now the quality of the mold is a key factor in determining how many cycles it will last. We could link the number of expected cycles to each of the four mold cost categories and arrive at a cost per cycle for each quarter of our quadrant. Again, it wouldn't be exact, but it would skew the cost in toward the right parts. What do you think so far?"

Marcella was even more surprised at Chris's grasp of the problem. "I'm still with you," she replied.

"We've got one more factor: the number of cavities. That we can't generalize. It's obviously a critical factor in arriving at a cost per part."

"Obviously."

"We'd have to use the exact number of cavities in each part's mold to come up with the cost, but we can use the average cost per cycle based on which of our quadrants the mold falls into." Chris hesitated for a moment. "Give me a half hour on my computer, and I'll put together an example. Can you do that?"

"Sure. I'll disappear for a half hour."

Marcella went back to her office, flopped into her chair, and sat there wondering how Chris had come up with such a simple answer in such short order. She remained there almost motionless until she noticed a half hour had passed. So she headed back into the plant.

"Check these out," said Chris as she entered. Chris laid his worksheets in front of her.

Key	Complexity/ Quality	Assumed Mold Cost	Estimated Cycles	Cost per Cycle
1	Low/Low	$5,000	5,000	$1.000
2	Low/High	$7,500	10,000	$0.750
3	High/Low	$15,000	25,000	$0.600
4	High/High	$18,000	40,000	$0.450

Part Number	Mold ID			Cost per Cycle	Cost per Part
	Key	Category	Cavities		
12345	1	Low/Low	4	$1.00	$0.250
12350	2	Low/High	2	$0.75	$0.375
12355	3	High/Low	6	$0.60	$0.100
12360	4	High/High	8	$0.45	$0.056
12365	2	Low/High	2	$0.75	$0.375
12370	3	High/Low	6	$0.60	$0.100
12375	1	Low/Low	10	$1.00	$0.100
12380	4	High/High	8	$0.45	$0.056
12385	3	High/Low	8	$0.60	$0.075
12390	2	Low/High	12	$0.75	$0.063
12395	1	Low/Low	6	$1.00	$0.167
12400	4	High/High	10	$0.45	$0.045
12405	4	High/High	10	$0.45	$0.045
12410	2	Low/High	6	$0.75	$0.125
12415	3	High/Low	8	$0.60	$0.075
12420	1	Low/Low	12	$1.00	$0.083

"Now the first worksheet," he explained, "takes the four quadrants of our matrix and uses an average mold cost and average expected life in terms of cycles to arrive at a cost per cycle for each category. That will be easy enough to come up with. The engineers and I can probably come up with good estimates in short order.

"The second example shows how we can create a simple worksheet where we can list the part numbers, select the mold category into which each best fits, and then enter the number of cavities in the mold to come up with a mold cost per part. That will take a little more effort because we have a lot of part numbers, but it is doable. I'm assuming this is something we'd only have to do once and then tweak it periodically since it's intended to reflect your 'long-term sustainable economics' and not the actual money spent each year."

"Wow!" Marcella was impressed. "Simple, doable, and it meets our objective of being reasonably accurate as opposed to being exact."

"Is there a spot in the costing software where we can include the mold cost per part?" asked Chris.

"I'm pretty sure there's a place for mold amortization that we can use. We don't use it now because we just stick the amortization in overhead, but I believe it's there and will work for us."

"Great! Then let's do it this way."

"How'd you come up with this so quickly?"

"I had an advantage over you," answered Chris.

"An advantage? What advantage?"

"I'm an engineer, not an accountant. I don't know about your accounting rules, and I don't care to know about them. As an engineer, I'm trained to see reality and then come up with a way to express it mathematically. Once I understood the constraints and learned about your two-by-two matrix gimmick, it wasn't too difficult to come up with a means of arriving at a good estimate within those constraints. You accountants are burdened by having a bunch of artificial accounting constraints wired into your brains. I'm not."

"I guess you're right," replied Marcella. "Let's go with this approach. I am going to have to do some thinking to figure out how I'm going to accommodate it on the books. We'll still need to capitalize the molds and amortize them on the books, and the amount of that amortization will undoubtedly be different from the amount we'll be including in product cost."

"Can't you do it the way you do overhead?"

"What do you mean?"

"Do the over- and under-absorbed bit. Record your amortization, and then absorb it based on how much we include in cost of sales. The difference is either over- or under-absorbed."

"I guess that will work. How do you know so much about absorption accounting?"

"I've had to explain manufacturing variances for years, so I figured I ought to learn how they're determined. So I studied up on that portion of cost accounting years ago. I found a good explanation in a book by some guy named Horngren. That way, I could come up with answers that made sense to you financial types."

"Well," said Marcella, "I think we're good. I'll write all this down and explain it to Alex. I have no doubt he'll like it. Can I have a copy of your worksheets?"

"Take these. I can print out another set if I need one."

"Thanks," said Marcella as she gathered up the worksheets and headed back to her office.

Chapter 26

M onday morning found the Admiral sitting across from Marcella ruing the fact that the weather had turned and his weekend golfing activities had wound down for the season.

"I'll probably play a little tennis," he said. "We've got some indoor courts at the club. But golf is my game. Leisurely pace, time to socialize, and enjoy the outdoors. You don't get that in tennis. Rachel and I are going to try to get away and head south once or twice this winter, and I can get in a few rounds then."

"Do you play tennis with Mr. Papasifakis?" she asked.

"Once in a while," he replied, "but he's not big into tennis. His game is golf. You'll be happy to know, though, that he and I still spend a lot of time together in the bar, talking about how much he likes accountants."

"Oh joy!" laughed Marcella.

"Did you and Chris get together and come up with a solution to our mold cost problem?"

"We did. And I think Chris nailed it. I'm amazed at how well he understands all this costing stuff. He even surprised me with some of the things he does know about accounting. I think he may just play dumb sometimes to see what I'm thinking."

"That's the Chris I've come to know since I've been here. He's one of those smart people who knows that the answers and opinions he has in his mind are only provisional based on what he knows so far, and that those answers and opinions can change as he accumulates more knowledge. Have you ever heard of Vaclav Havel?"

"The name is familiar, but I can't place it."

"Vaclav Havel was a writer and political dissident who later became the last President of Czechoslovakia and the first President of the Czech Republic. One of his most well-known quotes was, 'Follow the man who seeks the truth; run away from the man who has found it.' Chris is definitely a man who seeks the truth, not one who believes that he's found it."

"I agree. And he's a joy to work with."

"That's good to hear. Anyway, what have you two come up with?"

Marcella showed Alex the worksheets Chris had created and explained the reasoning behind them. Alex appeared pleased.

"Does this mean you've got a model for manufacturing done?" he asked after she had finished.

"I believe so," answered Marcella.

"Where do we go from here?"

"Jim will have to incorporate the manufacturing model into the Excel model he's creating to crunch the numbers and come up with the rates we'll be using. We've got to accumulate all the data we'll need to populate the model. We're going to have to determine how we're going to incorporate all of these changes into our ERP and cost accounting software as well as figure out how we're going to do the customer costing. We still don't have any add-on software to take care of that. There's a lot to do. But now we know where we're going."

"Any idea how long this is going to take?"

Marcella thought for a few moments. "Not having gone through this process before, I'm not too sure. We've got the holiday season coming up, and that'll undoubtedly delay things a bit. And I'm sure we'll encounter a few unanticipated roadblocks that we'll have to overcome. The best case would probably be three or four months."

"Well, hop on it. Let me know of anything I can do to expedite the process. I'm sure we're going to learn a lot of things about this company that we didn't know before when you're done."

"Will do," answered Marcella. "Make sure you emphasize the project's importance to IT, especially finding us software to assign customer costs. They tend to march to the beat of their own drummer."

"Understood," replied Alex, "I'll try to keep the fire lit under them."

Chapter 27

As had been the case before, Marcella didn't see the Major at the next IMA meeting until the meeting was breaking up. But there he was, in the lounge, with a Manhattan for himself and a glass of wine waiting for her.

"Any news to report?" he asked as she settled into the chair opposite him.

"I think we've solve the mold cost problem," she answered and proceeded to describe the session she had with Chris, the solution they came up with, and her discussion with Alex.

"I like it," smiled the Major. "You've incorporated the concept of 'long-term sustainable economics' well, and you've used the two-by-two matrix again to obtain accuracy where exactness would be overkill. Well done. It looks like you've got a good model for the manufacturing portion of the business."

"Now all we've got to do it implement the changes required to incorporate the new distribution and manufacturing models into our information systems," she replied somewhat sarcastically.

"That's true. Implementations are always difficult and take a lot of skill. But they're like the construction part of a building project. There are a lot more people with the building skills required to construct a building than there are people with the architectural skills required to design one that fits all of the owner's requirements. If the building is designed improperly, it doesn't much matter how well it's constructed; it will fail to meet the owner's needs. Most companies have the skills required to implement a costing system, but they don't have someone with your 'architectural' skills to figure out what they need to implement. Your company is fortunate that it has a finance person with a perspective like yours."

Marcella blushed. "I'm sure almost anyone in my position could have come up with a model that worked just as well."

"I disagree," exclaimed the Major. "I disagree strongly. Over the years, I've mentored many controllers and CFOs in the same way I've tried to mentor you, and in most cases, the results were disappointing. Most had trouble escaping from their bean-counter mindset and didn't want to put in the intellectual effort required to view the world as a forward-looking decision-maker instead of a backward-looking historian. Not only couldn't they think out of the box, they couldn't even recognize the fact that they were in a box. Mrs. DeCou, you've been a breath of fresh air for me."

"I've been?" she asked. "That's past tense. You don't mean ..."

"No, no," the Major interjected. "We're not done. We've only just begun."

"Whew! You had me worried for a moment."

"We've got a ways to go, if you're up to the journey."

"Count me in!" she answered. "You're right that there's a lot of intellectual effort required, but it's all worth it. I feel I'm a much more valuable member of PlumbCo's management team than I was at the beginning of the year. I even notice it in my day-to-day dealings with the other members of the team. They treat me more like one of them and less like an outsider just trying to keep track of what's going on and getting in their way when they want to do anything that costs money."

The Major laughed. "Tell me," he said, "did it occur to you that the thought process you went through in coming up with a way to handle mold costs might apply to another, even larger element of your company's costs?"

"No, not really," she answered. "What element is that?"

"You came to the conclusion that although molds are investments that require capitalization under accounting rules, they are really just irregular purchases required to maintain a particular product line. Amortization of the mold cost—which is a 'sunk cost' once you buy the mold—over a period of years in no way reflects the long-term sustainable economics of PlumbCo. To correct that problem, you came up with a model that more accurately reflects the true economics of the business."

"That's right."

"Can you think of any other element of cost for which that same logic might fit? Is there any other element of cost where you capitalize the cost and write it off over a period of years? Something even bigger than mold cost. Does your accounting for that element reflect the long-term economics of your business? Is that element of cost assigned to your products and services in a way that reflects its consumption by those products and services?"

"You're talking about depreciation expense, aren't you?"

"Yes, depreciation expense. Perhaps one of the most senseless concepts in managerial costing."

"Why do you say it's senseless?"

"You understand the concept of 'sunk costs,' don't you?"

"Yes. Sunk costs are costs that have already been incurred. The money has been spent and cannot be unspent."

"And you remember what your management accounting textbook said about sunk costs?"

Marcella hesitated for a moment and said, "Sunk costs are irrelevant."

"That's right. And what is PlumbCo's biggest sunk cost?"

"Probably our capital equipment."

"Now substitute 'capital equipment' for 'mold cost' in your logic."

"It's pretty much the same, isn't it?"

The Major looked at his watch. "It's getting pretty late," he said. "As I recall, there's no meeting in December because of the holidays, so we won't see each other again for a couple of months. And you've got a lot on your plate as you begin implementing your new warehousing and manufacturing models. So why don't you give this a little thought between now and our next meeting, and we can talk about it some more then?"

They both wished each other a Happy New Year and went their separate ways.

Chapter 28

Marcella was right in thinking that implementation of their new costing models would be slow during the holiday period. The folks in IT did find a software package that could extract data from the ERP system and assign distribution costs to customers. But they made no progress in determining how they could modify the existing system to accommodate the changes required to implement the new model for manufacturing. Although many of PlumbCo's managers took time off between Christmas and New Year's Day, Marcella liked to take advantage of the quiet time to get ready for the year-end work that dominated her time during January. As she sat in her office working, Jim appeared at her door.

"Got a few minutes?" he asked.

"Sure. I need a break from this drudgery. What's up?"

"I've been working on the model we'll need to calculate all of our new rates, and I wanted to bounce a few ideas off you."

"Sounds good. What have you got?"

"I've been reading up on cost models, and it's changed my perspective on how ours should be structured."

"I'm all ears."

"My original thought was to build an Excel worksheet that took our general ledger costs and assign them to the various activities for which we'll need to have rates. That would involve a multi-level structure with costs cascading down through interim activities until they end up in the activity that caused them. For example, we'd accumulate the costs of owning and maintaining the building and assign them to the activities that occupy the building—probably based on the square footage each activity occupies. We'd accumulate the cost of maintenance and assign it to the assets (mostly the building and equipment) that the maintenance department maintains. That would probably be done by getting estimates from the maintenance folks, using equipment hours, or some combination of the two."

"That sounds pretty logical."

"It does, but that would give us only the rates that were in the past, not the rates that would apply in the future. Although the historical rates might be useful in valuing our inventory, I'm not sure they would be useful in making forward-looking decisions."

"I see," replied Marcella. She thought for a moment and added, "Why don't we use the budget to populate your model?"

"That would be an improvement," replied Jim, "but I'm still not sure that would solve the problem. As I see it, the relevant cost for most decisions has nothing to do with rates. Most decisions require that we determine incremental costs. What's the impact of making a capital expenditure? What's the impact of adding or dropping a customer? What's the impact of a potential change in a process? Having rates based on history or our budget wouldn't be relevant to any of these types of decisions."

"You've got a point. Most decisions do require a calculation of incremental costs. When those types of decisions present themselves, I usually do a special analysis to support the proposed action."

"Does everyone always agree with your calculation?" asked Jim.

Marcella laughed, "Not always. Whoever is behind the proposed move usually thinks I'm being too conservative with my estimate of its impact. They want me to prove their proposal is the best use we can possibly make with our investment dollars. They like to nitpick every assumption I make."

"What if we could use the model to not only develop our costing rates, but to do these incremental cost analyses as well?"

"That would be great. How do we do that?"

"Make it a predictive model."

"A predictive model. How do we go about making a predictive model?"

"Based on what I've read, you should be able to take the factors you use to assign costs to cost objects—that's what they call the things you assign cost to like products and customers—to predict costs. For example, if we can forecast equipment uptime—the factor we use to assign equipment cost—we should be able to project the variable costs caused by that amount of uptime. The time the equipment operates drives the need for things like direct labor, utility cost, operating supplies, and maintenance materials. The labor required then drives the need for employees and costs related to employees, such as health insurance, payroll taxes, other employee benefits, and any supplies required to support the worker. If the equipment hours change, the model should be able to automatically determine the change in all of those costs. If any of the factors that link equipment hours to those costs change—like health insurance, utility rates, or the equipment's crew size—the model should be able to measure their impact."

"You think you can do that?" Marcella was pleased, but no longer surprised, by Jim's deep dive into his assignment.

"It's not really that complex. It may be a lot of calculations, but they're all simple $A \times B = C$ formulas, with C sometimes becoming the A for a follow-on computation. It's like a set of chain reactions set off by the original A. I diagrammed the chain reaction caused by equipment hours." He handed Marcella his diagram.

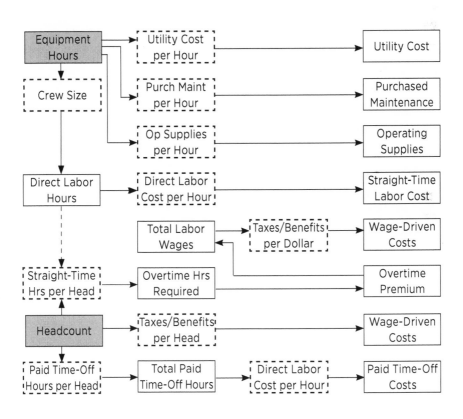

"The shaded boxes are the drivers. Those are the model inputs you would change to reflect the volume and mix of business we're modeling. They're the *A*s of our calculations. The boxes with the dashed lines are the inputs you would enter to reflect the relationships between the drivers and the costs. They'd be entered when you initially calibrate the model and would be changed only if the relationship changes. They're the *B*s of our calculations. The solid boxes are the costs calculated by the model. They're the *C*s.

"Once you enter the equipment hours, the model will use the 'per-hour' costs to calculate the utility, purchased maintenance, and operating supply costs. Once the equipment hours are multiplied by the crew size, the model determines the direct labor hours required. Multiplying by the direct labor cost per hour, it arrives at the straight-time labor cost. At this point, it gets a little more complicated. The direct labor required is supplied by a combination of straight-time hours and overtime hours. To determine the split between the two, we first need to know how many straight-time hours there are available per employee. To do that, we subtract the vacation, holiday, paid break, and other paid time off as well as absence hours from the base of 2,080 annual hours. By entering the headcount, we can then determine how many hours of overtime will be needed and the 50% overtime premium calculated. The headcount is entered as a variable so we can manage the assumed overtime percentage and keep it close to our company target.

"Once we've determined the overtime premium, we can add it to the straight-time wages to arrive at total wages. Multiplying total wages by any payroll taxes or benefits that are a function of total wages, we can calculate the total of those costs. With the headcount established, we can multiply it by any taxes or benefits that are a function of headcount to arrive at those costs. And finally, with the headcount and paid time off per employee hours, we can establish the total cost of paid time off."

Marcella sat in stunned silence.

"You figured this all out yourself?"

"Yeah, with a little coaching from some of the stuff I read."

"And you think you can incorporate this in the model?"

"Sure. It'll take some time, but it's all a bunch of $A \times B = C$ relationships. I figure the biggest drivers of our variable costs are equipment uptime and the drivers we've established for distribution. Line items, shipments, and such can drive the model's costs the same way as uptime. The other costs are pretty much either fixed or budgeted by management over any range of business we'd be likely to encounter in the near future. Things like depreciation, leases, indirect staff, or marketing costs could be entered directly.

"You can then use the model to calculate total company costs and costing rates under various volume and mix assumptions or change the affected factors to measure the change in total costs that would result from almost any management decision or action being considered. The change would be your incremental costs."

"James, you're amazing," said Marcella. She smiled. "Don't just sit there, do it!"

"That's all I needed to hear," he replied and headed back to his desk.

Chapter 29

The flurry of work in getting through year end usually kept Marcella from attending IMA meetings in January, but she didn't want to miss a chance to talk with the Major, so she took a break from her number crunching and headed to the Kingsley Arms on the appointed night. As had become the ritual, she headed to the lounge after not noticing the Major at all during the meeting. There he was, with a Manhattan in hand and a glass of wine waiting for her.

"Hope you had an enjoyable holiday," he said as she approached.

"Very enjoyable," she replied. "I hope yours was as well."

"No complaints," he answered. "Were you able to make any progress over the past two months?"

"Not much on the implementation. The IT folks found software to handle assigning distribution costs to customers, but they're still trying to figure out how to use it. Jim, my assistant, came up with a great idea for building our model so he could make it predictive."

"A predictive model, how interesting. What's his idea?"

Marcella proceeded to show the Major Jim's diagram and explain his idea.

"He came up with this himself?"

"I believe so. Apparently, he's done a lot of research into models and tailored something he thinks will be practical and fill our needs."

"He seems to have a pretty good head on his shoulders."

"That's certainly true. I thought we were hiring a capable young man, but I think we might have hired some kind of prodigy."

"Time will tell. By the way, did you have a chance to think about my comments last time?"

"You mean about applying the concepts we used with molds to our capital assets?"

"Yes, those comments."

"Not really. With the holidays and year end, I've been a bit negligent on that front."

"That's understandable. Unfortunately, you've still got to do the accounting part of controllership. That'll change before long."

"It will?" Marcella said with some surprise.

"All that accounting stuff is going to be fully automated. Recording transactions, making entries, closing the books, preparing standard reports, all that traditional accounting work will be handled by technology."

"So companies won't need a controller anymore?"

"No. I believe they'll need a 'real' controller more than ever. But that controller will be someone with a deep understanding of what all of the numbers mean and who can effectively interpret them for management. Interpretive and analytical skills will be much more important than bookkeeping skills. They'll need the kind of skills you—and, to a great extent, your right-hand man, Jim—have been showing this past year. Knowing how you did things in the past is important, but knowing how to do better in the future is even more important. Back in my day, 'cost accounting' was a new and valuable addition to management's catalogue of tools. Tomorrow, it will be 'profitability analytics': the ability to develop, interpret, and analyze both financial and non-financial information and create causality-based models that build robust, forward-looking scenarios and analyses. The focus will be on sustaining long-term value."

"That's quite a change," replied Marcella.

"But I'm glad to say you appear to be adapting to it quite nicely," smiled the Major. "Let's get back to those capital assets," he continued. "How do you treat them today?"

"We capitalize them as assets and then write them off over time using depreciation. For our manufacturing equipment, we use the straight-line method and an 8-year life."

"Does that make sense to you?"

"It does comply with accepted accounting rules, but based on our earlier conversation, I'm beginning to wonder if it really does make sense."

"How's that?"

"Well," Marcella answered, "there are two issues that jump out. One, it's all based on a sunk cost—a cost that most will agree is irrelevant. Two, it's backward looking. The profitability analytics idea that you talked about is forward looking. How does depreciation expense help us understand where we're headed? Does the amount we're recording reflect the economics of our business going forward?"

"So you think some base other than the original cost of the asset should be used? Some more forward-looking base?"

"Yes. Maybe something like replacement cost."

"That's an improvement. Are you going to replace all those capital assets with new models of the same assets that you have now?"

Marcella thought for a minute. "Maybe not. The way technology is advancing, there may be new types of equipment in the future to perform the same processes that our existing equipment does now. In those cases, we'd most likely replace the current asset with a different kind of asset."

"So replacement cost might not be the ideal substitute for original cost?"

"Perhaps not. We should probably consider what type of equipment we might purchase in the future to replace the capability we have now with the current equipment. In some cases, it would be a new model of the old asset, but in other cases, it might be something completely different."

"That's an excellent thought. It focuses on the future, on the long-term sustainability of your business. How about the mechanics of measurement? Would you take the cost of purchasing that asset in the future and apply the same mechanics that you do for depreciation?"

"I can't see why I wouldn't."

"You'd record the same amount each year for 8 years and then nothing after that? And what if, after using one amount for a few years, you discover that a new type of asset with a different cost will be the most likely candidate for replacing the existing asset?"

"Now that you mention it, recording the same amount each year doesn't sound too logical. After all, for our manufacturing equipment at least, the need to replace it accrues as it is used, not as chronological time passes. There should probably be more cost recorded if we used the equipment 4,000 hours in a year than if we used it only 3,000 hours."

"So you might want to consider a different method?"

"Yes, I think some other method might be in order."

Just then, Marcella's phone rang. "It's my husband," she said. "Looks like we're running late again tonight, and he's probably wondering when I'll be home."

"He'd be right. We are running a bit late. Better tell him you're about to head home. Why don't you give this some thought—discuss it with Jim, he might have some good ideas—and we'll pick it up again next month."

Marcella agreed, and the two headed their separate ways.

Chapter 30

Marcella's phone rang. It was Kelsey Hayes, PlumbCo's director of sales.

"Hi, Gabby," answered Marcella, "what's up?" "Gabby" was a nickname Jake Ullrey had given Kelsey when she was hired as a sales representative a decade ago, and to her chagrin, the name stuck. It wasn't really a description of her personality; Jake was just a fan of old westerns and jumped at the chance to refer to one of his employees as "Gabby Hayes," the character actor who appeared in so many of those films. As a new employee, Kelsey didn't object at the time, and as the years wore on, she got used to the folks at the office calling her "Gabby." She did hope, however, that with Jake no longer on site every day, folks would get back to calling her by her real name. Marcella sympathized and usually called Kelsey by her real name, but she slipped every once in a while and reverted to the nickname.

"If you've got some time today, I'd like to talk with you about the customer profitability measures you're working on."

"How about now?" replied Marcella.

"That would be great. I'll be there in 5 or 10 minutes."

Ten minutes later, Kelsey arrived and settled into one of Marcella's visitor chairs. After the two exchanged pleasantries and talked for a few minutes about personal matters, Kelsey brought up the reason for her visit.

"Jim and Rich have been talking with me about the work they're doing to better understand how fulfillment costs impact customer profitability, and I wanted to make sure I fully understood what they were doing and how it would eventually impact me and my sales staff."

"That's understandable," said Marcella. "I probably should have gotten you involved in the process already, but this has been a new undertaking for me, and I didn't want to get too many people involved until I was sure of where we were going. My initial concern was to develop the numbers correctly. I didn't want to give the folks it might impact any false impressions due to my lack of experience in the area."

"That was probably a wise approach. I'm not upset at not being involved, just curious. I figure it might change the way we deal with our customers and that I ought to begin preparing for that change. Are you comfortable talking about it now?"

"I think so. I've had a few conversations with Alex, as well as a very experienced costing expert I met through the IMA; and, although I'm sure I haven't reached a high-level expertise, I think I'm able to discuss the topic with a lot more confidence than I had when we began."

"What's the IMA?" asked Kelsey.

"It's the Institute of Management Accountants, an international association of accountants in industry. We have local chapter meetings each month, and one of the members is an elderly gentleman who obviously has an extensive amount of experience in managerial costing. He has taken me under his wing and helped guide me through the process."

"That must have been a lucky break for you."

"It sure was. But that's one of the benefits of being an IMA member. The networking opportunities, especially those you develop through your local chapter, are outstanding. You can often find someone who's already 'been there and done that' who is willing to help you in an area where you don't yet have experience. In my case, he found me. He overheard me talking with other members about my dilemma, and he volunteered his assistance."

"So, what do I need to know?"

Marcella proceeded to describe the work she'd done with Rich and Jim and the type of information they expect to gain from the development of rates to attach warehousing and fulfillment costs to customers. She also gave Kelsey a "heads up" on the possibility of changes in measuring the cost of the company's individual products.

"These changes could be pretty comprehensive," said Kelsey. "The product costs we've been using might have been inaccurate, and the costs we previously treated as either manufacturing overhead or SG&A will now be linked to specific customers."

"That's right," replied Marcella. "It could give us a totally different picture of how and where we make money."

"It'll probably affect our list prices," said Kelsey.

"Aren't they based on the market, not cost?" asked Marcella.

"They're based on a combination of market and cost. We do market studies to arrive at a 'probable market price' for each of our products and compare those 'probables' to our product costs. In a majority of the cases, the margins shown for the product meet our target, so we go with the 'probable' for our list price. When the margin doesn't meet our target, we use some judgment. If it's a product with limited demand, we'll usually go with the 'probable' because we're not going to sell many of them anyway; they're just there to make our product line complete. If it's a product with significant demand, we may bump the price up some, but it will depend on whether we believe the higher price for the item will risk having a customer source their entire order elsewhere because the list price of one or two items is too high. Even in those cases, we can usually take care of the problem with a discount. It'll still be applied to the higher list price, so we'll be better off than discounting the lower 'probable.' The process isn't formal or scientific; it's based on our experience and intuition."

"Do you ever use a list price lower than the 'probable'? Like when the apparent margin is exceptionally high? Might the lower list price of those items attract some customers?"

"No. I don't recall us ever using anything less than the 'probable.' The fact that no customer ever really pays list price anyway means that our list prices are really just a starting point for negotiation. Unless, of course, it's a small customer—the kind of customer that uses the standard volume discount schedule and doesn't negotiate."

"So what we will have," said Marcella, "are different product costs to compare against your probable market prices. My guess is that the results of those comparisons will be quite different once we've revised our product-costing practices. However, I don't believe that is where our changes will have the biggest impact on your selling activities. I believe its impact will be biggest in your discounting practices."

"On our discounting practices?"

"Yes. As I understand it, your discounts are based almost exclusively on sales volume. The more the customer buys, the bigger the discount."

"That's usually the case," replied Kelsey. "There are some exceptions, but that's the norm."

"What I think we'll learn, however, is that customer behavior has a significant impact on how much of the sales price is eaten up by the cost of storing, picking, packaging, and staging their orders. Picture the difference in those costs between two customers with the same sales volume: one customer who orders 10 of the same fast-turning product and another customer who orders 10 different slow-turning products. For the first customer, we didn't store the product very long and only had to go to one spot in the warehouse to pick the product for shipment. For the second customer, we stored each product for quite some time and then had to go to 10 different places in the warehouse to pick it. The work required to fill that second customer's order will erode more of the margin earned on the sale than the first customer's."

"I see what you mean. Volume will probably still be a factor, but we may have to include other factors in our discounting practices as well."

"That's the way I see it. Obviously, you know a lot more about the market as well as customer perceptions, expectations, and likely reactions than I do, but it does appear we'll have to somehow take these 'order fulfillment' costs into account when we establish an appropriate discount for each customer."

"That'll be a big change. I'm not sure any other supplier does anything like it."

"I'm sure you'll figure out the best way to incorporate this new information into your pricing. That's why they pay you the big bucks."

They both laughed.

"Now that you've brought this up," added Kelsey, "there's another thing that might need to be factored in."

"What's that?" asked Marcella.

"The amount and type of work we do in marketing to our various types of customers. We put a lot of effort into marketing to our larger customers—you know, the big-box stores and retail chains. As a matter of fact, even non-marketing people get involved with them. Chris sometimes gets involved when they have manufacturing questions and Rich gets involved with distribution issues. Their purchasing people can demand a lot of our time. On the other hand, small customers simply read our ads, come visit our booths at trade shows, and place orders. That's about it. There's very little one-on-one marketing done with them. Those pre-sale activities may have an impact on customer profitability as well."

"Good point. I hadn't thought of that. I'm going to have to figure out how we might capture those costs and assign them to customers as well."

"I'm just trying to make both of our jobs more difficult," laughed Kelsey.

"Well, we've both got more to think about now. I'll keep you posted on our progress in coming up with the rates and a way to assign them to customers. You can give some thought to how you're going to incorporate the new information into your discounting practices."

"Sounds like a plan," said Kelsey.

Chapter 31

Christian Scheele's phone rang. It was Marcella.

"Got some time for me?" she asked.

"For you, I'll make time. Your office or mine?"

"I'll come there." Ten minutes later, Marcella was settled in across from Chris.

"How can I be of service to my favorite controller today?" asked Chris.

"You no doubt remember our discussions about mold costs? Well, we've got some similar long-term sustainable economic issues with the cost of our capital equipment."

"You mean depreciation isn't a good measure?" Chris laughed.

"What's so funny?"

"I thought that might come up. The way accountants do depreciation always seemed pretty stupid to me."

"Why is that?"

"Well, I don't know much about accounting, but ..."

Oh crap! thought Marcella, *whenever someone starts out with a statement like that, it usually means they do know a lot about whatever accounting topic they're about to complain about.*

"But," continued Chris, "it always seemed to me that the way you accountants handle depreciation expense is pretty dumb. First, you start with a 'sunk cost.' I did learn about sunk costs and how they're irrelevant when reading that Horngren book I mentioned earlier. Second, you arbitrarily pick a period over which to write off that irrelevant cost from the menu of allowable asset lives. Finally, you arbitrarily pick one of the many allowable depreciation methods from the menu of allowable methods. Once you've got those three things identified, you use them to arrive at a fixed annual expense for owning and operating a piece of equipment even though the equipment is not consumed by the passage of time, but by its being used. Why on earth would the expense be the same when I operate a machine for 2,000 hours as it is if I operate it for 4,000 hours? A piece of equipment's life is measured in hours or cycles, not chronological time."

"You mean it's related to run time, not earth orbits around the sun?" interjected Marcella.

"That's a good way to put it."

"I must admit I got that expression from Jim. He used it when he was explaining how he was incorporating maintenance expense into our cost model." She paused for a few moments then asked, "By the way, if you don't know that much about accounting, how do you know so much about accounting?"

Chris laughed. "Really, I don't know that much. But as an engineer, I try to figure out ways to turn physical realities into something that's measurable. What you accountants do with depreciation is pretty obvious to anyone who has had to deal with budgets and explain operating results to their boss. It's simple and easy to understand. But to someone like me, who doesn't care about what the accounting authorities say, it makes absolutely no sense at all. By the way, that's just a polite way of my saying 'it's stupid.'"

Again, Marcella was impressed at Chris' grasp of the issue. "So how long have you felt this way about depreciation?" she asked.

"Oh, probably 10 years or more. You know, engineers and operations people think a lot of the things accountants do are pretty questionable. But whenever we bring up our concerns, we're told 'those are the rules. We have to do it that way.' So we just shut up and get on with our jobs." He looked at Marcella with a big smile on his face. "You know, you're the first finance person I've met who's willing to talk about this stuff without falling back on the excuse 'those are the rules.'"

Marcella blushed a bit. "I'm afraid that if you and I were having this conversation a year ago, that's what I would have told you."

"So something's changed your attitude in the past 12 months?"

"Yes. Let me put it this way: I've learned that the financial information decision-makers need is like an elephant."

"An elephant?" asked Chris. "I think I see a metaphor coming."

"Yes, an elephant," Marcella replied. "And accountants are like a blind man given one chance to touch the elephant and then describe what it looks like. Because the description the accountant comes up with is then written down as rules and regulations that must be followed in reporting to outsiders, it becomes 'gospel' and taken to be the only correct picture of the elephant. What I've learned is that there are many parts to an elephant that just one touch won't reveal, and decision-makers need to understand the entire elephant, not just the part the accountant touched."

"Nice. I like that. Let me give you another. Light travels in a wide range of wavelengths, from the short wavelengths of infrared to the long wavelengths of ultraviolet. Somewhere in between the two is a small stretch of wavelengths we call 'visible light,' which is the light we can see with our eyes. Until infrared and ultraviolet light were discovered in the nineteenth century, we assumed that visible light was all the light there was. Accountants saw that visible light, developed ways to measure it, and have continued to use those measurements even after the other wavelengths were discovered. Unfortunately, decision-makers need to measure light along the entire spectrum if they're going to make informed decisions."

"That's the second time you've used light and the spectrum as a metaphor."

"It's just the frustrated scientist in me. I really wanted to grow up to be a theoretical physicist, but I ended up being an engineer managing a molding plant. I am glad, however, that you've ventured into the infrared and ultraviolet. Now what are we going to do about depreciation?"

Marcella related the conversation she had recently had with the Major.

"I like the way he thinks," said Chris. "We need to somehow look into the future and predict our capital needs and turn those into a cost-per-run hour of the existing equipment so we can accumulate the funds to make those purchases when the need arises. That's how we can sustain our existing capital base in the long term. Hmmm ..." Chris hesitated.

"Something wrong?" asked Marcella.

"No, a question just popped into my head that I was trying to quickly answer myself."

"What's the question?"

"Let's say we have a major piece of equipment that will need to be replaced in about 3 years. It has about 10,000 hours of its original 45,000-hour life expectancy remaining, and we run the thing about 3,000 hours per year. A replacement will cost us $450,000. So after about 9,000 hours of additional run time, we'll need to spend $450,000 on a replacement unit. Does that mean we'll need to include $50 per hour in the cost of running the equipment so we've accumulated the money to buy a new unit after 9,000 hours?"

"No. That's not how I see it working. We probably wouldn't sell many of the parts made by that equipment anyway if we included that $50 per hour in its cost. I see the 'long-term sustainable' concept for long-lived capital equipment reaching out decades, not years. We need to make sure we're covering the cost of having the capability this capital asset provides us indefinitely. It could involve replacing it multiple times during that span. Based on your example, if we include $10 per hour in the equipment's hourly costs and operate it 3,000 hours per year, we'd reflect the cost of replacing it every 45,000 hours of usage."

"That makes sense, but it's going to be hard to find a crystal ball that will enable us to look that far into the future."

Marcella thought for a moment. "You remember a few months back when I mentioned 'Oxenfeldt's Rule'?"

"You mean the one that says something like, 'An error in estimating the magnitude of an effect usually is far less serious than mistakes due to wholly overlooked consequences?'"

"That's the one. Well, one of the things I picked up reading Oxenfeldt's book was the fact that in decision-making, when you don't forecast something using a valid model with assumptions, you are still forecasting it subconsciously; you just don't realize what model or assumptions you're using. As a consequence, you can't tell how valid your assumptions were as the future unfolds or why it's coming out different from what you had forecast. You can't correct something when you don't know how you created it in the first place.

"For example, take your piece of equipment," she continued. "If we used it 3,000 hours per year since its purchase, it's about 12 years old. If we bought it for $360,000, we'd have recognized $45,000 of depreciation in each of the first 8 years and included $15 per hour in its cost. For the past 4 years, we would have recognized no depreciation at all. There would have been no depreciation in its hourly cost. It wouldn't have dawned on us that there was a problem because we hadn't used a valid model with assumptions to come up with the amount in the first place. There would be no 'red flag' to tell us there was a problem or what bad assumption led to that problem.

"But if we had a valid model for projecting our future capital requirements and monitored it regularly, we could continually adjust the assumptions to reflect changes in technology, our strategy, the market, or any other factor that impacts what we need to maintain our existing capabilities."

"So," replied Chris, "we need to come up with a valid model for sustaining our capital base and some assumptions with which to populate that model. Right?"

"That sounds right to me," replied Marcella. "However, I am still going to have to do our financial accounting in terms of 'visible light.' The way we measure some costs for decisions won't be the same as we report them on the books. For example, the product costs used for pricing decision won't be the same as we use for cost of goods sold."

"We're already going to do that for mold costs, aren't we?"

"That's true. Alex, the Board, and the bank are going to have to understand what we're doing. I'm pretty sure Alex and the Board will get it. I'm not so sure about the bank. Bankers live in the visible light."

"Tell you what," said Chris, "I'll get with the engineers and some of my key manufacturing folks and come up with a long-term capital model for our core equipment, estimate the cost for purchasing capital assets to maintain our existing capabilities, and develop a set of lives for each item in terms of run hours. When I'm done, we can take a look at it and see what kind of impact turning depreciation into a 'capital preservation allowance' might have on our costs."

"Capital preservation allowance, eh? I like that," said Marcella. "Let's call it our 'Capital Preservation Allowance.'"

Chapter 32

Several months had passed since Jim Stinson described his approach to creating a predictive cost model to Marcella. Since then, he'd kept her posted on his general progress, but he hadn't given her a lot of details or a demonstration of his creation. The lack of detail didn't bother her. Marcella had developed a great deal of confidence in Jim's ability and thought it best to let him create the model without any interference or predetermined timetable. In a sense, he was "going where no man (or woman) had gone before" and needed to be given the space to put his ideas to the test and make the required adjustments in his thinking as he progressed. Also, Marcella figured she didn't have much to add. She was still amazed at what Jim came up with through his own industry and research.

She was working on finishing up her management reports after the February close when her phone rang. It was Jim.

"Hey, boss!" he said, "think you'll have some time this week to go over the cost model?"

"How much time do you think we'll need?" asked Marcella.

"It's hard to tell. There's a lot to go over. Two to three hours maybe."

Marcella looked at her schedule. "I should have all this month-end stuff done by Wednesday. How about we meet Thursday morning?"

"We'll need to use the conference room," said Jim. "That way, I can project the model onto the screen, and we'll have plenty of room to spread out printed copies of some of its more important sections."

Marcella checked the conference room's availability. "It looks like it's open Thursday morning. I'll reserve it for us from 9:00 until noon."

"Great! I'll be ready for you then."

When she arrived at the conference room on Thursday morning, Jim was there waiting with his computer connected, files booted up, and printed copies ready.

"Before we get into the Excel model itself," said Jim, "let me explain a little about its overall structure. We'll start with its most basic form." He put a diagram on the screen.

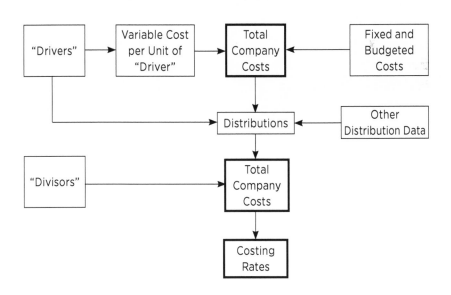

He continued, "The first thing we want to do is accumulate the total cost of operating the company at any given volume and mix of activity. I see those costs as either being 'driven' by measures of our activity level—things like equipment uptime hours and line items picked—, budgeted for a relevant range of activity, or fixed. The measures like uptime or items picked I refer to as 'drivers,' because they actually drive the amount of cost we incur. The budgeted items include things that are usually defined as step-variable or semi-fixed, like material handling or purchasing, which are 'driven' by some measure of activity, but I don't see it worth complicating a model for a company our size with all the data and calculations necessary to make them 'driven' costs. They're going to be fixed over a pretty wide range of our activities, and we can finesse them if we think we're going out of the relevant range. Other budgeted items would include things that vary based on management decisions, such as advertising and special projects. Fixed costs would be items like property taxes, leases, and the like."

"That makes sense," interjected Marcella. "It's pretty much an expansion on the idea that costs are either fixed or variable."

"That's right, but the added dimension is that we identify and then calibrate the right 'drivers' to be able to accurately project those variable costs as the driver measurements change. Which brings me to 'calibration.' In the diagram, we must calibrate the variable cost per unit of driver. What's the electricity usage per each machine's hour of uptime? How does uptime impact the required production labor hours? Or how do line items picked affect the hours required from warehouse workers?

What's the health care cost per employee? Those are the kinds of 'per unit of driver' measures we'll need to establish."

"That sounds like a pretty daunting task. We don't measure utility consumption by piece of equipment or have standards for picking orders. We'll have to get a lot of people involved in pulling all this information together."

"I'm not so sure of that," answered Jim. "Remember, we're trying to be accurate, not exact."

"I think I'm supposed to remind you of that," laughed Marcella. "How do you propose coming up with all of the calibrations?"

"I look at it this way: These are all $A \times B = C$ calculations. For historical periods, we should know most of the As and Cs. If we solve for B, we've arrived at the cost per unit of A. Assuming the historical period gave us a representative sample, we should be able to use those Bs to project future costs."

"But we don't always know the Cs in a lot of detail," objected Marcella. "For example, electricity expense isn't measured by machine; it's a single monthly invoice that is charged to one account. How do we figure out the C for each different type of equipment?"

"Consumption units," answered Jim.

"Consumption units?" replied Marcella. "What the heck are consumption units?"

"I thought you might ask that." Jim handed Marcella a worksheet.

Machine	Uptime Hours	Relative Consumption	Consumption Units	Utility Cost per Uptime Hr
Machine A	2,000	1.0	2,000	$3.00
Machine B	2,000	2.0	4,000	$6.00
Machine C	2,000	3.0	6,000	$9.00
Total Consumption Units			12,000	
Total Utility Cost			$36,000	
Cost per Consumption Unit			$3.00	

Machine	Uptime Hours	Utility Cost
Machine A	2,500	$7,500
Machine B	2,000	$12,000
Machine C	3,000	$27,000
Total Utility Cost		$46,500

Machine	Uptime Hours	Utility Cost
Machine A	1,800	$5,400
Machine B	2,200	$13,200
Machine C	2,400	$21,600
Total Utility Cost		$40,200

"Let's suppose we have three machines that each ran for 2,000 hours last year and the utility bill for those machines was $36,000. That's 6,000 total machine hours or $6 per hour for utilities. However, we know that they don't all consume utilities at the same rate. Machine C requires more utilities per hour than Machine B, and Machine B requires more per hour than Machine A.

"Now we can have our engineers go out and study the consumption rates in detail, or we can estimate their 'relative' consumption per hour. If the machine that uses the least utilities uses 1.0 consumption unit per hour, how many units per hour would each of the other machines use? In the example, since Machine *A* uses the least, we'll give it 1.0 consumption unit per hour. Using that as a base, our operations and engineering folks can give us their best estimate of the relative consumption of the other two machines.

"In the example in my worksheet, they estimate Machine *B* uses twice the utilities per hour as Machine *A* and Machine *C* uses three times as much per hour. We can then multiply those relative consumption unit estimates by the uptime hours to arrive at a total consumption unit figure, which we then divide into the total utility costs to calculate a utility cost per consumption unit. That will then enable us to establish a utility cost per hour for each piece of equipment. You can see from the two examples at the bottom of the worksheet that we should get a relatively accurate measure of utility costs as uptime hours change."

"Excellent!" exclaimed Marcella. "And another use of the Major's 'weighting' idea."

"Yup," said Jim. "That's what suggested the method to me. I saw how you used weights in distribution and figured they'd work here as well."

"You've got me convinced. We can calibrate the model's driven costs using a representative historical period and solving for the *B*s. What's next?"

Jim drew her attention back to the diagram on the screen.

"Now that we've accumulated the total cost of operating the business, we need to distribute some of those costs in such a way that they can be incorporated into the rates that we use to assign our costs to products and customers. Visually, it looks like this." Jim flipped the screen to another diagram.

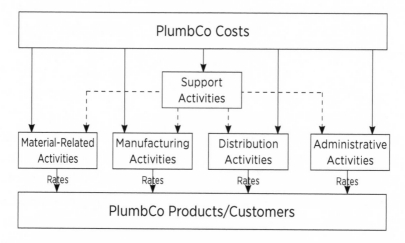

"On this diagram, I've divided the work we do into five categories of activities: material-related, manufacturing, distribution, administration, and support. The first four categories will end up with rates we can use to assign their costs to products and customers. The fifth one will not. Support activities are there to support the activities in the other four categories. That's why I called them 'support' activities. Pretty creative, huh?"

"Oh, quite imaginative," answered Marcella with a grin.

"These support activities need to be assigned to the other activities using some basis that reflects their demand for the support activities' work. The dashed lines represent this distribution of the support activities' costs to what you might call their 'customers.'"

"What basis do we use to distribute them?" asked Marcella.

"I see two types of distributions: statistical and analytical. The *statistical distributions* are based on hard data that has either been entered into the model or calculated inside the model. For example, I used square footage occupied to distribute the cost of owning and maintaining the building. Headcounts are used to distribute human resources. Equipment hours are used to distributed machine maintenance. These are done automatically within the model.

"In contrast, *analytical distributions* require the direct input of distribution percentages. Many of these distributions could be done statistically if we chose to make the model much more complex. If we were a much larger organization, it might even be worth doing so. For example, we could use data like invoices paid, invoices sent, payroll checks processed, and so forth to distribute accounting costs, but that seems like overkill for a company our size, so the model I built just requires that we enter an estimate of how much of accounting's time relates to each of the other activities."

"You've given this a lot of thought, haven't you?"

"I guess you could say that. There's a lot of information on the internet that talks about various ways to attack the construction of a cost model. People have been throwing around ideas for improving cost information for nearly 30 years, and I feel like I've read them all. Your brain can get all tangled up going through all the ideas, but I found a few key fundamentals that I kept in mind in building the model."

"And those are?"

"The first one is *causality*. The model must be based on cause-and-effect relationships. The second is *accuracy*. The information generated by the cost model needs to be close enough to economic reality that it does not mislead decision-makers. Precision is not a goal of the model. Lastly, *simplicity*. Users are going to have to believe in the numbers generated by the model. If it's too complex, they won't understand it well enough to have that confidence."

"Well said," responded Marcella. "Now let's finish off your diagram."

"Okay," said Jim, flipping the screen back to his original diagram. "We've got all the costs accumulated into activities that we will convert into rates that can be used to assign those costs to products and customers. To do that, we need to divide each activity's accumulated cost by its base. Some of those bases were used to drive those costs in the first place. For example, equipment uptime was used to project the cost of operating the equipment as well as the number of direct labor hours that will be required to support its operation. Those are the 'drivers' that are already in the model and can be used to arrive at a cost per equipment or direct labor hour.

"However, there are other bases that will be used to assign costs that were not used to drive them in the model. Set-ups are a good example. We have five set-up people per shift. That number is not driven by the number of set-ups. It's one of those budgeted costs I mentioned earlier. So we need to enter the number of parts produced by set-up type, as well as the weights we're giving to each type of set-up, to establish the set-up cost per part. In the diagram, I refer to those as 'divisors.' They're not used to drive the cost, but they are used to turn the cost into costing rates. At the end of the process, we have our product and customer costing rates."

"So, based on the model you've created, we'd be able to measure incremental costs by modifying the inputs and then comparing the before and after total accumulated costs?"

"That's correct."

"And we'd be able to develop costing rates based on any volume and mix of business, as long as it sits somewhere within the relevant range supported by the non-driven costs?"

"That's right on as well."

"I think I'm going to like this model," said Marcella. "Okay, I've got the big picture, now walk me through the details."

Jim proceeded to walk Marcella through the details of the Excel model schedule-by-schedule. When they were done she exclaimed, "Whew! That's a lot of number crunching. But it's all a lot of fairly simple $A \times B = C$ calculations. It's understandable in concept, and the math isn't all that difficult to understand either. I think we'll be able to get the troops to believe in the numbers when all is said and done."

"I hope so," replied Jim.

"Now that you're nearly done with the model, how'd you like to change it?"

"Change it?"

"Not so much change it, but expand it."

"How so?"

Jim listed intently as Marcella described her recent discussions with Kelsey Hayes and Chris Scheele.

After thinking for a few moments, he said, "I think I can see a fairly easy way to incorporate the customer issues Kelsey described in the model. We can set up separate activities to collect the costs of supporting the various types of customers. I believe she mentioned big-box stores, retailers, and small customers. Relevant support activities, like Sales & Marketing, Engineering, and Customer Service, can distribute the appropriate percentage of their cost to each customer and those totals divided by the cost of the products sold to each activities' customers to arrive at a percentage add-on rate. It'd be sort of like a customer-specific G&A rate."

"That sounds like it would work," said Marcella, "and easy enough to understand. See any problem in working the plumbing into your Excel model?"

"Nope. It's a pretty simple add-on."

"Great! Now what do we do about this Capital Preservation Allowance?"

"I do have a question about that concept. Having a forward-looking cost per hour for preserving our production assets is clear enough, but what about the non-production assets? Do we use traditional depreciation expense for them, or do we substitute a forward-looking cost per year?"

"Excellent question," replied Marcella. "What do you suggest?"

"Well," Jim answered, "if we're using forward-looking rates for preserving our production assets, it seems to me that we should do the same for non-production assets. It would probably remain a cost per year, but that cost would not be financial depreciation. Instead, the cost would be an estimate of the amount we need to accrue to sustain whatever capability the non-production asset provides."

"Will including a Capital Preservation Allowance for either the production or non-production assets in your Excel model pose any problems?"

"It shouldn't. The non-production asset allowances are just another fixed annual cost for each activity, and the production ones are basically another variable cost driven by uptime, like electricity. Come to think of it, I can put a 'switch' in the model that will enable us to use either depreciation expense or the Capital Preservation Allowance in calculating rates. You might still want to use the depreciation numbers when doing any analyses that need to agree with the financials."

"That sounds like a great idea." Marcella paused for a moment and then asked, "Do you think of everything?"

Jim laughed. "No, I'm sure there's a lot I've missed. But I have been doing a lot of research, and it gives the outside world the impression that I actually know what I'm doing. I've tried a lot of things that didn't work too well before I arrived at this edition of the model. You just haven't seen all my screw-ups."

"Well," Marcella interjected, "get to it and add the new items to your model."

Chapter 33

It had taken almost six months, but the warehousing and IT folks had worked along with Jim to implement the new software for assigning warehousing costs to customers. Jim had provided a set of "provisional" rates for distribution activities—rates they would use until the whole-company cost model was completed. He anticipated that these rates would change to some degree when all of the company's costs were included and distributed in the model.

Before going over the first reports generated by the new system with Alex, Marcella thought it best to discuss the results—and the implications of those results—with Rich Vivian and Kelsey Hayes. Her goal was to make sure they both had a chance to give the numbers a good "smell test" before presenting them to Alex as well as discuss the impact those numbers might have on their decision-making. The last thing she wanted was for there to be any debates over the results or misinterpretations of the data when they all met with Alex.

Marcella, Rich, and Kelsey all assembled in the conference room where Jim had already set up to present a summary of the results.

"We finally got some numbers to look at?" asked Rich as he sat down.

"Yes, finally," answered Jim. "It's taken a lot of time and effort, and the numbers are still subject to change when we complete the entire model, but I think they're close enough to provide us with some interesting insights."

"First of all," added Marcella, "you've got to keep in mind that the manufacturing costs have not yet been updated. The product margins that we'll show are based on the old manufacturing model, which we know is incorrect. What we want to focus on today is the impact distribution costs have on measuring a particular customer's—or customer group's—profitability. In other words, how much the distribution costs erode the product margin on goods sold to a customer or group of customers."

"Understood," replied both Kelsey and Rich.

Marcella turned to Jim. "James, the floor is yours."

"The first things we'll look at," began Jim, "are the costing rates for each of the distribution activities. Here's a summary of those rates."

Put-Away	$0.20	per unit
Storage Cost per Group A Unit	$0.05	per unit
Storage Cost per Group B Unit	$0.20	per unit
Storage Cost per Group C Unit	$0.60	per unit
Telephone Order Cost	$55.00	per order
Mail/Fax Order Cost	$27.50	per order
Electronic Order Cost	$13.75	per order
Picking Cost Per Group A Unit	$2.40	per line item
Picking Cost Per Group B Unit	$3.00	per line item
Picking Cost Per Group C Unit	$3.75	per line item

Loose Box Shipment Cost	$12.00	per box shipped
Full Box Shipment Cost	$8.00	per box shipped
Pallet Shipment Cost	$24.00	per pallet shipped
Return/Restock Cost	$65.00	per return

"As you'll recall, there were six basic activities we decided were important to understanding distribution costs: putting away the product, storing the product, processing orders, picking the product, shipping the product, and handling returns and restocks. For storage, order handling, picking, and shipping, we broke the activity into three categories based on the level or resource of work involved and came up with different rates for each of the three categories using the 'weighting' process."

Jim then went on to show what costs went into each of the activities and how they had been converted into the rates. Both Rich and Kelsey raised several questions during Jim's discussion, but he was able to allay their concerns by showing them exactly how the costs were accumulated in the model and by explaining the source and nature of the assumptions made. All eventually agreed that the rates passed "the smell test" and fairly reflected the cost of the activities they represented.

"Before we go any further," interjected Marcella, "let me ask a question. Is there any insight provided by this schedule that we could use to improve the business?"

"Not that I think I could use," answered Kelsey. "I need to see how they affect my customers first."

"How about you, Rich?" asked Marcella.

Rich thought for a few moments. "Well, before today, all of my costs were just a big pool of warehousing costs. Now that they've been broken down into measurable costs for each major warehousing or distribution activity, I could probably address each one and see if I can find ways to reduce it. Jim's got the details of what makes up each one, which will help me understand why each activity costs what it does."

"That's an excellent idea," replied Marcella. "You might even be able to use some of the data to develop performance indicators that you could use in managing the warehouse."

"That's right. I'll have to give it some thought, but I think you're on to something there."

"Okay, Jim. Carry on."

"I thought," said Jim, "a good way to get a feel for the implications of assigning these distribution costs to customers would be to select two small, two mid-sized, and two large customers and see how distribution costs impact their profitability." He projected his worksheet on the screen. "I've given each customer an alias so we would only pay attention to the data and not let any of our feelings for the particular customer affect our discussion. The first two columns, Alpha and Beta, represent those 750 customers that make up 15% of our sales. Gamma and Delta represent the 85 customers that make up 25% of our sales, and Epsilon and Zeta represent those 15 customers that make up 60% of our sales.

"The data in the schedule is pretty self-explanatory. They represent the number of units purchased and orders placed by each customer as well as the line items picked, orders shipped, and returns handled for each one. You can see how they vary between the two customers in each category."

Customer Ordering Information	Alpha Industries	Beta Corporation	Gamma Products	Delta Distribution	Epsilon Supply	Zeta & Sons
Units Purchased:						
Group A	268	101	2,208	2,020	30,123	24,803
Group B	56	102	1,104	915	14,988	17,432
Group C	10	150	382	721	4,921	7,435
Total	334	353	3,694	3,656	50,032	49,670
Orders Placed:						
Telephone Orders	0	12	0	0	0	0
Mail/Fax Orders	12	0	0	52	0	52
Electronic Orders	0	0	12	0	52	0
Total	12	12	12	52	52	52
Line Items Picked:						
Group A	18	7	147	270	1,000	885
Group B	6	10	110	181	750	875
Group C	2	30	76	302	500	750
Total	25	47	334	753	2,250	2,510
Packages Shipped:						
Loose Box Shipment	3	15	0	37	0	0
Full Box Shipment	22	10	0	270	0	2,100
Pallet Shipment	0	0	26	0	350	170
Total	25	25	26	307	350	2,270
Returns Total	2	2	5	10	6	12

"Yeah," said Kelsey, "you can see how Alpha buys primarily our Group *A* products while Beta buys more of the slower-moving items. Or how Gamma sends us one electronic order monthly while Delta mails one in every week. Interesting stuff."

"But wait until you see how it impacts profitability," added Jim as he switched to a new slide.

Customer Value Analysis	Alpha Industries	Beta Corporation	Gamma Products	Delta Distribution	Epsilon Supply	Zeta & Sons
Sales	$2,400	$2,800	$36,940	$42,300	$520,000	$480,000
Cost of products sold	$1,488	$1,680	$22,533	$25,803	$338,000	$302,400
Product Margin	$912	$1,120	$14,407	$16,497	$182,000	$177,600
% to Sales	38.0%	40.0%	39.0%	39.0%	35.0%	37.0%
Customer support costs:						
Put-Away	$67	$71	$739	$731	$10,006	$9,934
Storage	$31	$115	$560	$717	$7,456	$9,188
Order	$330	$660	$165	$1,430	$715	$1,430
Picking	$67	$159	$971	$2,324	$6,525	$7,562
Shipping	$212	$260	$624	$2,604	$8,400	$20,880
Returns	$130	$130	$325	$650	$390	$780
Customer Support Cost	$837	$1,395	$3,384	$8,455	$33,493	$49,773
Customer Margin	$75	($275)	$11,022	$8,042	$148,507	$127,827
% to Sales	3.1%	−9.8%	29.8%	19.0%	28.6%	26.6%

"Here, we cost out those warehousing and distribution activities and see how they eat into each customer's product margins. Now remember, the product margins themselves are still suspect, but the customer support costs are pretty darn accurate.

"The two small customers, Alpha and Beta, are quite interesting."

"Yeah," interjected Kelsey. "Alpha's sales and margin percentage are lower than Beta's, but Alpha's profitability is a lot greater."

"And you can see why," added Rich. "Alpha purchases items we've had to hold in inventory longer; their people place telephone orders, which are quite costly to process; they have fewer units per line item picked, which means we have to do more work to pick their orders; and they require a lot more of the expensive loose-box shipments. It all adds up, doesn't it?"

"Maybe we should dump Beta as a customer," suggested Kelsey.

"Or maybe not," replied Marcella.

"But we're losing money on them," protested Kelsey.

"That doesn't necessarily mean we'd be better off without them than with them."

"I don't understand."

"The data on this schedule shows that they aren't a high-value customer in our portfolio of customers, but we won't know if we're better off without them than with them unless we understand how much our overall costs will decrease if we don't sell to them. If overall costs decrease by more than $2,800, we're better off without them. But if they decrease by less than $2,800, they're still making a contribution to our bottom line, at least in the short run. We wouldn't want many customers like them, but for the time being, we're better off with them.

"You see, not all of the $3,075 of cost will go away if we no longer sell to them. As a matter of fact, the only costs that will disappear will probably be the variable cost involved in manufacturing their products. We'll still have the same warehouse staff, and fixed manufacturing costs will remain the same. The impact of dropping such a small customer won't affect those costs. If there were a significant group of small customers like Beta, the result may be different. Dropping the entire group might enable us to reduce costs more than the sales loss, but not just this one. You certainly don't want to make a habit of adding customers like Beta. That would eventually lead to adding more cost in the warehouse and, perhaps, to our fixed manufacturing costs. Once we get the entire model built, we'll be able to do these 'incremental' types of calculations."

Kelsey still looked confused. "Then what good does this information do for me?"

Marcella smiled. "Remember our conversation a few months ago?"

Kelsey laughed and said, "Refresh my memory. It's not as good as it used to be."

"You can use it to find ways to make them a more valuable customer. Perhaps you can convince them to order quarterly instead of monthly. That'll reduce the order processing and probably the picking cost as well. With fewer orders for the same volume of business, the number of parts per line item will probably increase, which will reduce the picking cost attributable to them. Getting them to order by mail, by fax, or electronically will reduce the cost attributable to them even further.

"Jim, do me a favor. Go to your worksheet and see what would happen if you had them order electronically once per quarter and cut the number of line items picked by two-thirds and see what happens."

Jim did as requested, and the result surprised everyone. Beta's ordering cost was reduced by $605 (from $674 to $55), and its picking costs fell by $106 (from $159 to $53)—a total decrease of $711. Beta's $275 loss turned into a $436 profit.

"So you see, using the data to find ways to alter customer behavior can lead to more profitable and valuable customers. Doing it for only one customer won't do much, but using it to modify the ordering behavior of a significant number of customers will either enable us to reduce costs or open up capacity so that we can fill more orders at no increase in cost."

"Well, I'll be," said Kelsey. "I might even be able to offer additional discounts to get the customers to change their ways."

"That's a possibility," replied Marcella. "Think about how you can use this data in your pricing strategies, and be sure to mention them to Alex when we meet with him."

"Let's look at the other customers on Jim's analysis." Kelsey was indeed interested.

The conversation continued along the same lines for another hour as both Rich and Kelsey began to see the possibilities with this newfound information. As the meeting broke up, Kelsey said, "This isn't just an accounting exercise, is it? This is valuable and actionable information we can use to improve PlumbCo's performance." Rich agreed wholeheartedly.

Chapter 34

Marcella was working on her April closing when her phone rang.

"Hey Marcella, it's Chris."

"Oh, hi, Chris. What's up?"

"Remember our discussion about a capital preservation allowance for the production equipment a few weeks back?"

"Of course."

"Well, I've got some numbers for you. Got a minute or two to go over them?"

"Sure. Give me a few minutes to wrap up what I'm doing, and I'll come over to your office."

Fifteen minutes later, Marcella arrived at Chris' office.

"Sorry it took so long," said Chris. "I can give you all the usual excuses, but they don't really matter. I should have gotten this to you weeks ago."

"You haven't been holding anything up," replied Marcella. "Jim's just now getting our cost model in good enough shape to begin loading data. In that sense, you're actually early."

"Regardless," smiled Chris, "I shouldn't have taken this long." He slipped a schedule across his desk toward Marcella. "I met with my people, as well as people from Engineering, to discuss the type of equipment we'll be buying in the future, figure out what its price might be, and estimate what kind of life each category of equipment might have in terms of run hours. The schedule in front of you summarizes our conclusions."

Marcella studied Chris' analysis and asked, "Is the price we'd pay for each category of equipment the same amount we'd pay if we bought it today?"

"Yeah, I didn't want to complicate the issue for our discussions. I figured you and I could adjust those amounts if it was necessary. We did, however, decide that we would most likely be replacing the existing equipment with the same type of equipment. Technology might make new machines better, but they'd be the same type of machines: molding presses, shearers, and rotary heat sealers. Some new technology might come along that totally changes those processes, but we didn't think it likely."

Description	Presses			Shearing	Packaging
	Under 75T	75T-125T	Over 125T		
Estimated Cost	$60,000	$100,000	$150,000	$30,000	$50,000
Estimated Life (in Hours)	30,000	30,000	30,000	45,000	35,000
Capital Accumulatoin per Hour	$2.00	$3.33	$5.00	$0.67	$1.43

"That sounds fine. I think using today's dollars is okay. This is an amount that we'll be reviewing and revising each year based on whatever new information comes along. And we are 'Oxenfeldting.'"

"Oxenfeldting. That's a new one to me. What's Oxenfeldting?"

"We're estimating something that we need to know if we're to understand the economics of our business. We're not omitting it from our model or substituting a precisely measured but irrelevant number like depreciation expense. We're complying with Alfred Oxenfeldt's Rule. Hence, we're Oxenfeldting."

"If you say so," laughed Chris.

"How about the estimated lives? Where did those come from?"

"They're a combination of our past experience and the estimated hours that vendors promise when they're trying to sell the equipment. We started with the vendors' numbers and then discounted them based on what we've experienced."

"Well, if they look good to you, they look good to me. We'll go with them and see if anyone—meaning Alex—takes exception to them once they're incorporated into the model. Thanks for all your help."

"No problem. I'm getting antsy to see how this all comes out."

"Me, too!" replied Marcella.

Chapter 35

"What's new on the costing front?" asked Alex as he settled down in Marcella's office early one Monday morning. "We've been discussing it in 'dribs and drabs' over the past few months, but I'm not sure where we stand right now."

"As you probably know," answered Marcella, "the last pieces of a project are always the hardest to pull together. Just when you think you see the light at the end of the tunnel, another issue comes up or some new aspect of the problem you're solving becomes apparent. That being said, I think we're getting close to having a full cost model that fairly reflects our operation as a manufacturer and distributor.

"The main issues since you and I last talked about this at length have been developing measures that provide a more insightful and valid measure of our ongoing capital needs than depreciation expense; creating a cost model that is predictive, not just descriptive; and determining what to do with the information we'll be getting from the model. I think Jim's pretty much done constructing the model itself and has been working with Rich, Chris, Kelsey, and the IT folks to collect and load the data we need to calibrate the model and create an initial set of costing rates. The IT folks assure me that they've made the changes necessary to incorporate all of the new concepts and rates into our MRP and cost systems."

"What was your decision on replacing depreciation expense?" asked Alex.

"Chris and I developed an idea we call a 'capital preservation allowance.' It's designed to ensure that we're generating the cash required to preserve our existing manufacturing capability over the long term." She then went on to explain how she and Chris went about the process and how Chris developed hourly costs for preserving the manufacturing assets.

"So you guys have decided that your 'preservation allowance' should be a variable cost per hour, not a fixed cost per year—at least for the manufacturing equipment. I often wondered why accountants acted as if time, not usage, was the way to link the cost of manufacturing assets to their use. Looks like you had that question as well."

"The question was mostly the result of Chris thinking like an engineer. As we talked about it, I began to realize that the way accountants treat the cost of capital assets is primarily driven by the fact that it's easy and consistent. They need to spread the amount paid for the asset over the financial periods it benefits, so they come up with one-size-fits-none rules so that everybody does it the same. I don't know if those creating the rules actually cared whether or not the resulting numbers represented any kind of economic reality, but over the years, accountants just began assuming that they did. Well, as I now understand, they were wrong."

Alex then changed the topic. "The idea that the cost model will be predictive, not just descriptive ... how is it predictive?"

Marcella pulled Jim's diagrams from her files and showed them to Alex.

"The costs of operating our business are either 'driven' by some activity measure, budgeted, or fixed. To make the model 'predictive,' we needed to make costs vary by an appropriate amount whenever the causes—or 'driver'—of the driven costs change. The driver of manufacturing costs is equipment uptime. It's the operation of the equipment that requires a certain amount of labor hours, utilities, purchased maintenance, and operating supplies be expensed. The labor hours driven by the equipment's uptime then drive the direct labor cost as well as paid time-off benefits, purchased fringe benefits, and payroll taxes. So you can see equipment uptime drives most of the variable manufacturing costs.

"On the other hand, in the warehouse, variable costs are driven by the number and type of warehousing events that take place: the number of parts put-away, orders picked, shipments prepared, and returns handled. Those drive the amount of warehousing labor time that is required, which, in turn, drives the labor cost, benefits, and payroll taxes.

"We set up the model so that these measures would drive the appropriate costs, and then we used last year's actual results to calibrate the model."

"What do you mean by 'calibrate' the model?" asked Alex.

"The driven costs can be looked at as $A \times B = C$ calculations. If we know what A was last year, and we know what C was last year, we can solve for B and use it as the relationship between A and C—in other words, the relationship between the driver and the resulting cost. Solving for B is what I mean by 'calibrating' the model. For our initial run of the model, we'll assume that relationship is representative. As time goes by, we'll test the relationship and adjust it as necessary."

"Okay," said Alex. "And the rest of the costs?"

"The rest of the costs are either budgeted or fixed. They are simply entered into the model and assigned to the appropriate activity center. For example, budgeted costs like legal, outside accounting, and promotions would be assigned to General Management, Accounting & Finance, and Sales & Marketing, respectively. Fixed costs like property taxes or leases would be assigned to the activity center where the property being taxed or asset being leased resides. When using the model for 'what-ifs?', the fixed costs would remain the same over an extended range of business volume, while the budgeted, or discretionary, costs would be subject to change based on management's judgment."

"Sounds pretty solid," said Alex. "I'll be interested in seeing its results and how we can use the model's predictive abilities to support our decisions. Speaking of which, how do your peers feel about using the output of the model to support their decisions? Do they appear confident that the information will be accurate and relevant for them? Do they have any ideas as to how they can use the information to improve the business?"

"Rich, Chris, Kelsey, and I have had several discussions about the use of the model's output. At the outset, they weren't sure what they'd do with it, but they never raised any question—to me at least—as to whether the information would be accurate. They seemed pretty confident that the model's results would be valid."

"I think I know why," interrupted Alex.

"Why the model's results would be valid?"

"Yes. I believe their confidence stems from the fact that you involved them in creating the model. You took the time to ask questions about how their arenas operate, what issues they face, and how they think their portion of the model should be designed. You took their input, devised a way to model their arenas, and then gave them a chance to critique your ideas. You didn't impose a model on them; you facilitated their creating a model of their arena that you could incorporate into an overall company model. The model is their baby as much as yours. That's why they have confidence."

"I guess you're right. But that's not why I did it that way. I did it the way I did because I had only a superficial knowledge of distribution, manufacturing, and marketing. There's no way I could have designed a model that reflects the realities of our business without their cooperation and input."

"You'd be surprised at how many people design various kinds of business models without involving those who know the most about what is being modeled. But that's another story. How about the model's use? What do they say about that?"

"You know," replied Marcella, "the first thing people think about when it comes to costing at a manufacturer is calculating product costs to value inventory and calculate cost of goods sold. They might then extend their thinking to use it as guidance in establishing prices and understanding product and customer profitability. The first change here was that we began to see the need to understand both product and fulfillment cost if we are to properly establish prices and measure customer profitability. The revelation was that costing models don't exist solely to cost products. They have other uses as well—uses that can help us improve the business.

"We all agreed that the more accurate, relevant, and granular information we'll get from our new cost model will provide us with measurable insights that we've never had before. So we needed to start asking ourselves, 'How can these insights and their measurements help us do better in the future?'

"To get started, Jim and I met with Rich and Kelsey to go over some of the preliminary results of the distribution portion of the model. We wanted to give them a chance to "scratch and sniff" the preliminary numbers as well as begin thinking about how the numbers could help them improve the organization. Rich was pretty quick to mention that by breaking down the work of the warehousing personnel into distinct and measurable activities, warehousing was no longer just a single pool of costs. He then understood not only the cost of each key step performed in the distribution process, but what resources were involved in those costs. He saw this as information that would enable him to better control and reduce those costs in the future."

"Excellent," interjected Alex. "I'm glad to see Rich has bought in."

"Yes, I wasn't sure about Rich early on, but he's shown a great deal of interest in the process as we've gotten deeper and deeper into it."

"How about Kelsey? Did she see any way to use the information in her arena?"

"After a lot of discussion, she began to see how she might be able to improve the profitability of customers by encouraging them to change their ordering practices—especially those smaller customers where the product margins are pretty much eaten up by the cost of fulfilling their orders. After Jim ran some examples showing the impact of ordering practices on customer profitability, Kelsey came up with the idea of offering additional discounts to some customers when we can show the fulfillment savings would be greater than the additional discount allowed."

"And Chris?" asked Alex.

"We haven't presented any preliminary numbers to him yet, but I'm not worried about Chris," replied Marcella. "He always seems one step ahead of me when it comes to costing. I wouldn't be surprised if he doesn't already have plans for using the new information to improve manufacturing."

"Sounds like we've made a lot of headway, both in coming up with better cost information and in understanding how we can capitalize on that information."

"I believe so," replied Marcella, "but we've still got to reach the finish line. Those last few steps can generate some surprises and prove to be the most difficult."

"Well, keep me posted, and let me know if there's anything I can do to keep things moving."

Chapter 36

It was the last IMA meeting before the summer break. Marcella and the Major had continued to meet after each month's meeting, but their discussions were mostly updates on PlumbCo's progress. The Major hadn't raised any new issues since he suggested they consider a different means of accounting for capital assets in January.

Marcella updated the Major on Jim's progress in creating the predictive model and gave him a summary of the discussions that led up to their development of the 'capital preservation allowance.' She also told him of the discussion she had with her peers about how they could use the output of the model to improve the business.

"I like it," said the Major when she was done. "You've not disappointed me. Jim's model appears to be solid, your capital preservation allowance appears to solve the depreciation expense problem, and you've been getting all the key players involved in the process. When you're done, the new cost model will be theirs, not just yours, and they'll be more likely to put its output to good use."

Marcella was pleased, and to some extent relieved, that the Major approved of their efforts.

"I've got one more thing for you to think about," added the Major.

"What's that?"

"What do you currently do with your general and administrative expenses? Do you assign them to your products and customers in any way?"

"Not in our day-to-day accounting. They're just 'below the line' expenses in our normal financial statements. When we look at product and customer profitability, we add them as a percentage on top of all the other assigned cost."

"So if the total product and customer cost equals $10, you add the percentage to the $10?"

"That's right."

"Does that make sense to you?"

Marcella figured the Major was up to something and said with a smile, "I guess I must think so since that's what we do. But since you're asking," she added, "I assume you don't think it's such a great idea."

"Tell me," he asked, "what does your 'general and administrative' expense represent?"

After thinking for a few moments, she answered, "It's the basic cost of managing the other activities of the business and doing the general things required to be in business, like complying with all the rules and regulations, dealing with bankers, submitting tax returns, and so forth."

"So you're saying that 'G&A' makes it possible to perform all of those company activities that can be assigned to products and customers? And that's why you add it as a percentage to the total?"

"That's pretty much it."

"What if you have two products that cost $10 to manufacture: one that's $2 of material and $8 of PlumbCo's assignable activity cost; and another that's $8 of material and only $2 of its assignable activity cost? Your method of assigning G&A costs is telling me that the general and administrative effort required to support the production of both products is the same, even though one product requires four times more activity cost than the other. Does that make sense to you?"

"Not the way you've put it. If we do four times more work to manufacture a product, you'd think we should assign four times more of the cost required to support those manufacturing activities."

"That's right," said the Major. "If the cost of the material triples, you'd still do the same amount of work to manufacture the product. The same would be true if the material was provided at no cost. You'd do the same amount of work. Why would material cost have a bearing on the amount of effort required to administer the production of the product?"

"So you're suggesting that when it is necessary to assign general and administrative costs, we assign them as a percentage of ... ?" Marcella hesitated.

"Cumulative activity cost," interrupted the Major. "All of the other activity costs that have been assigned to the product or customer. The percentage would be higher, but the base smaller and more appropriate for the costs being assigned."

"I can see that," replied Marcella. "G&A is there to support the performance of the company's other activities, so it follows those activities to cost objects."

"Cost objects? Where did you pick up that term?"

"Jim uses it to describe the things you want to know the cost of—like products and customers."

"It's a pretty common phrase used in that sense. 'Cost objectives' is preferred by some, but I'd say most refer to them as cost objects. Tell me," the Major continued, "does our discussion about assigning G&A costs suggest anything else to you?"

"Anything else? Not really."

"Is there any other calculation you do that uses total cumulative cost—including material—as a base?"

Marcella thought for a moment. "Not that I can think of. The only cost we tack on as a percentage of all the other costs is general and administration."

"How about something other than costs?"

"Other than costs?" Marcella was confused. "I think you've lost me."

"How do you come up with target margins for your products?"

"We mark up the manufacturing cost about 60%."

"The total manufacturing costs?" asked the Major.

"Yeah, the total."

"Including the material cost?"

"Including the material cost," answered Marcella.

"So you do have something else for which you use total cumulative cost—including material—as a base."

"I guess you're right. We use it as a base for setting target prices."

"I'll ask you the same question I've asked several times already: Does that make sense to you?"

"No it doesn't," declared Marcella. Then with a smile, she added, "But only because you asked me the question. You don't ask that question if it does make sense. However, I'll admit that at the moment, I can't explain why it doesn't make sense."

"Financially speaking, what is the ultimate goal of a for-profit organization?" asked the Major. "What does the owner of a for-profit organization hope for in return for his or her investment?"

"The obvious answer is that the owner wants a superior return on the investment: one that's better than he or she could get investing in something else of equal risk."

"In this case, the obvious answer is the correct one. Now tell me, how does one calculate the return someone gets on their investment?"

The answer was simple, but Marcella hesitated for a moment as she considered whether this could be another one of the Major's trick questions. "You divide the annual value generated by the investment—in terms of interest or profit earned or the increase in the investment's value—by the amount invested. In simple terms, it's profit divided by investment."

"Good. Now, is that the financial goal of PlumbCo? Does your owner seek to earn a superior return on his investment?"

"Of course," answered Marcella. "I'm sure he has a lot of other goals for the company, but those other goals are made possible by the attainment of a superior return on his investment in the company."

"So, if the goal of the company is to earn a superior return on investment, why do you use a different measure to determine how well the various components of the business help it meet that goal?"

"I'm lost again."

"You use a 'percentage of investment' to measure the company's goal, but you use a 'percentage of sales' target to set your target prices and determine how well each product, customer, market, or other subset of the business helps to meet that goal."

Marcella protested, "But we don't use a percentage of sales target. We mark up each product's manufactured cost by 60%."

"Think about it," replied the Major. "Measuring anything as a percentage of sales is just another way of adding a percentage to total cumulative cost. Adding 60% to your total manufactured cost is the same as targeting a 37.5% gross margin percentage. Your definition of a customer or product that helps you reach your goal is one with a gross margin percentage of 37.5% or more. Your overall company goal is apples, but you evaluate the parts that make up the company by measuring oranges. Why is there such a mismatch? Why don't you use the same basis for both?"

"Because no one ever questioned the practice," Marcella answered sheepishly. "I'd never really given it a second thought. Everyone uses 'percentages of sales' to measure things. They're always talking about profit and gross margin as a percentages of sales. You just accept it as the norm and don't ask questions. But now that you've pointed out the inconsistency, it doesn't make any sense. You're right. We ought to use the same method for both. To really see how well a product or customer helps us reach the company's financial goal, we need to figure each product's or customer's return on investment."

"Unfortunately," replied the Major, "that's easier said than done. Assigning investment to each product or customer would be a pretty complicated process. An alternative would be to embed an appropriate weighted average cost of capital—one that includes the owner's target return on investment—in each activity's cost. That way, the rolled-up cost of each product or customer would represent the revenue you need to realize for that product or customer to meet the company's return on investment goal. But that probably adds more complexity than you'd want to incorporate into your model at this time."

"So what should we do?"

"There is a simple surrogate measure you can use. It's not perfect, but it is many steps closer to reflecting a customer's or product's value to the company than any percentage of sales measure."

"And that is …"

The Major laughed, "I was going to tell you. The measure is profit as a percentage of value added. It's another way of looking at a markup of cumulative activity cost."

"What does that accomplish?" asked Marcella.

"Break your company's cost into two categories. There are the materials, parts, and services you purchase from outside parties, and there are the activities you perform to sell, manufacture, and distribute your products. To which of those two groups would you attribute most of PlumbCo's investment—the stuff you buy from outsiders or the work you perform internally?"

"Well," answered Marcella, "off the top of my head, I'd say less than 10% of our investment is tied up in direct materials, and the rest is used in manufacturing, storing, and distributing products."

"So would you say that most of PlumbCo's investment is being used in the performance of its various business activities?"

"Yes. I believe that's true."

"Now let's go back to the two $10 products I used as examples earlier: one being $2 of material and $8 of activity cost and the other $8 of material and $2 of activity cost. Which of these two products do you think would have tied up more of your investment? The one where you added $2 of activity cost or the one where you added $8 of activity cost?"

Marcella's face brightened as she began to see where the Major was leading her. "The one where we add $8 of activity. As a matter of fact, the investment would probably be 4 times more than for the product with only $2 of activity cost."

"Does that suggest anything to you with regard to the profit that should be expected on these two products?"

"I'd say we should require 4 times more profit on the product with $8 of activity cost than we do on the one with only $2 because we're tying up 4 times more investment." At that point, the issue started to clarify itself in Marcella's mind, and she began thinking out loud. "By measuring profit as a percentage of either activity cost or value added, we eliminate the distortion caused by passing through the cost of direct materials in the sales price. We could establish target prices by coming up with a percentage to add to activity cost that would enable us to reach our company return on investment target. In our financials, we would highlight the percentage return on either activity cost or value added, not sales. It wouldn't be perfect, but we'd be a lot closer to pricing our products based on their return on investment and representing our performance in our financials."

The Major looked at his watch. "Oh, we've run rather late tonight," he said. "We'd better wrap up for now." He stood up to leave.

"That's probably a good idea," replied Marcella. "My brain is spinning while trying to get this all organized in my head." She laughed. "I don't think I could handle any more new ideas tonight anyway."

Chapter 37

"James," said Marcella as Jim Stinson settled himself into the chair opposite her, "I've got some good news and some bad news. Which do you want to hear first?"

"Give me the good news first," he answered. "Maybe the good news will make the bad news not seem so bad."

"The good news is that I've gone over your modeling ideas with Alex and the Major, and they both were quite excited about them."

"And the bad news?"

"You'll have to tell me how bad it is, but we're going to have to make a change to your model."

"What kind of a change?"

"During our last conversation, the Major pointed out the irrationality of assigning our general and administrative costs to products and customers as a percentage of total cost."

"Irrationality?" said Jim. "Isn't that how everyone does it?"

"I believe the vast majority of companies do, but that doesn't mean it makes sense. Let me walk you through the Major's argument." Marcella then briefed him on the Major's rationale for discrediting the common practice and his rationale for using either value-added or total activity cost as a basis for assigning G&A costs.

"So, to put in another way," said Jim, "G&A is attributable to converting the vendors' materials into products and then selling and distributing those products. It has nothing to do with the materials purchased from those vendors, so it should not be attributed to them."

"Well put," replied Marcella. "The word 'attributable' is a perfect word to use to explain it."

"I can't take all the credit," laughed Jim. "I picked it up reading the IMA's Statement on Management Accounting on the conceptual basis for managerial cost models. It talks about traceability and attributability. *Traceability* is when something can be identified with a specific output based on verifiable transactions—such as routings, bills of material, time reports, and so forth. They're said to have 'strong' causality. *Attributability* is when something is traceable in a non-linear, non-quantitative manner to other work activities or outputs. They're said to have 'weak' causality, but causality nevertheless. In this case, G&A is attributable to all of the company's other activities. Ergo, link G&A to the other activities."

"It sounds like you've already thought about this."

"Not exactly. I've had the principle lodged in my brain since I read the SMA, but I hadn't thought of it applying to our G&A costs. Probably because I hadn't thought to question the usual method. But now that you've brought it up, it's obvious. My question is, 'Why does everyone do it the wrong way?'"

Marcella smiled. "Probably because the method for linking G&A to cost objects has no impact on financial accounting. G&A is just a pool of costs that appears 'below the line.' No one has really given it any thought. However, there is a more important ramification of the Major's thinking."

"And what is that?"

"How do we usually measure a product's or customer's profitability?"

"We look at its profit as a percentage of its sales."

"See any problem there?"

Jim thought for a few moments. "This has got something to do with looking at activity costs versus total cost, doesn't it?"

"You're on the right track," replied Marcella. "What do we remove from total cost to arrive at total activity cost?"

"Material cost?" answered Jim uncertainly.

"That's right. And what do you have when you subtract material cost from sales?"

"I believe that would be value added."

"Does that suggest anything to you?"

Jim sat silent for several minutes. His expression then changed from one of confusion to one of enlightenment. "Are you saying that we should measure profitability as a percentage of value added?"

"Either that or a percentage of activity costs." She then repeated the rationale behind the Major's argument that profit as a percentage of sales is dysfunctional if the company's objective is to attain a superior return on investment, as well as his case for using activity cost or value added as a base that more closely reflects a product's or customer's return on investment.

"Makes a lot of sense to me," said Jim.

"Now tell me, what kind of a change does this mean you'll have to make in the model?"

"I don't see much problem in the model. It'll be pretty easy to change the basis for the G&A rate. Should I use activity cost as the base for the customer rates as well?"

"I hadn't thought about that," replied Marcella. "We're selling value added to the customer as well, aren't we? We should probably use it there as well."

"That's a little more work," said Jim. "We'll need to include a percentage breakdown of activity cost among the customer categories. That might be difficult." After thinking for a few moments, he added, "If we believe the proportions would be about the same, we could use the sales breakdown instead. That should get us pretty close, and, considering the Oxenfeldt principle, it might be close enough for our purposes."

"So you're telling me the bad news isn't so bad?"

"That's right. It'll probably take me only a few hours to make the changes."

"Then what are you waiting for? Hop to it!"

"Consider it done."

Chapter 38

As it does to most projects, summer slowed down the progress on the cost-modeling project. Key sources of input were off on vacation at the most inopportune times, and even Jim was gone for two weeks on his own well-deserved vacation. Finally, one day in late August, Jim stuck his head in Marcella's office.

"Hey, boss!" he said, "Got a couple of minutes?"

"Sure," she answered. "I've got one around 9:32 tomorrow morning and another one at 3:37 next Thursday afternoon."

"Okay," Jim laughed, "let me rephrase my question. Do you have 15 to 30 consecutive minutes you could dedicate to meeting with me sometime in the near future, preferably today?"

"Would right now work?"

"You bet," answered Jim and he handed her a memory stick. "Boot up the file named PlumbCo Cost Model v.1." She did as instructed, and the upper left-hand corner of PlumbCo's cost model appeared on her screen.

"You finished it!" exclaimed Marcella. "You've finished the model?"

"I believe so. I got the last of the data I needed from Chris a couple of days ago, and I've been checking and re-checking my formulas ever since. I've also done a little smell-testing of the results, and they seem to make sense to me. But then again, I'm just an accountant. We'll have to see what the kahunas think when they see the results."

"What time period does the data in the model represent?"

"I used the 12 months ended June 30. I wanted it to be more current than last year's data, so I went from mid-year to mid-year."

"Okay. Now take me through it. I want to see how you got all those features you talked about into this thing."

"That might take more than the 30 minutes I asked for," replied Jim.

"You've got the rest of the day if you need it." Marcella pushed the papers she was working on aside and gave Jim her full attention.

Over the next three hours, Jim took Marcella through the 37 schedules and 3,000 lines that made up the Excel model.

"It's really pretty simple, isn't it?" said Marcella when they were done. "I'm sure it wasn't simple thinking it through or getting all the data collected, but the model itself—it's not all that complex."

"It had to be pretty simple. I built it," laughed Jim.

"Don't undersell yourself," replied Marcella. *"La semplicità è l'ultima sofisticazione."*

"What does that mean?"

"It's something Leonardo da Vinci once said that has stuck with me all these years. It means 'Simplicity is the ultimate sophistication.' I believe Einstein once said something to the effect that any intelligent fool can make something complicated, but it takes a touch of genius to make something complicated simple."

"Does that mean I get a raise?"

"Let's not go that far."

They both laughed.

"However, I do have a few questions."

"I thought you'd have more than a few," replied Jim. "Shoot."

"On Schedule RI-01. You take the equipment operating hours, multiply them by the crew size, and then add a 20% indirect activity allowance to arrive at the labor hours required. Explain the 'indirect activity allowance' again and how you got the 20%."

"In a perfect world, you should be able to take equipment operating hours, multiply them by the size of the crew that attends the equipment when it operates, and arrive at the total labor required to operate the equipment. However, we don't live in a perfect world. We usually have a few extra people around to make sure we have enough of them available to run production each day. The workers are still around when the machine is down temporarily. Sometimes, the crew is actually larger than normal. There are a lot of reasons we might have more workers than the simple formula 'equipment uptime multiplied by theoretical crew size' would indicate. If we're going to be able to accurately predict the amount of production labor we'll need, we must account for those extra hours. That's the purpose of the indirect activity allowance. It grosses up the 'perfect-world' calculation to be a 'real-world' calculation."

"And how did you arrive at the 20%?"

"The 'perfect-world' calculation predicted we'd need 65,150 hours of labor to support the production level during the year. We know, however, from the accounting records that we actually paid for 78,180 hours. That's 20% more than theoretically required. Hence, the 20% indirect activity allowance."

"Can you calculate our savings if we cut that 20% in half?"

"It might take a few seconds, but I can."

"A few seconds?" replied Marcella with astonishment. "This I've gotta see."

"First, you change the 20% on Schedule RI-04 to 10%." Jim typed the changes into the model. "Then you check the bottom of the schedule's second page to see how your supply of labor matches its demand. The 40 FTEs required when the indirect allowance was 20% now provide more labor than we need. If we reduce the headcount to 37, it results in the need for about 6% overtime, which is just about the same level we were at with

INCREMENTAL ANALYSIS   Schedule IA-01
PlumbCo, Inc.   10:09 AM   5-Jan-20

| | Total Activity Costs | | Increase |
	After	Before	(Decrease)
SALARIES AND WAGES			
Salaries	$2,150,720	$2,150,720	$0
Hourly	$2,605,013	$2,709,253	($104,240)
Paid time-off benefits	$259,700	$269,108	($9,408)
Overtime shift premium & special comp.	$114,352	$122,842	($8,490)
TOTAL SALARIES & WAGES	$5,129,785	$5,251,923	($122,138)
FRINGE BENEFITS			
Purchased Benefits and Taxes	$1,685,033	$1,729,530	($44,497)
OPERATING EXPENSES			
Depreciation	$297,500	$297,500	$0
Cost of capital	$0	$0	$0
Leases and rentals	$26,000	$26,000	$0
Utilities	$238,679	$238,679	$0
Purch maint. & supplies	$466,400	$466,400	$0
Administrative supplies	$319,700	$320,000	($300)
Other fixed and budgeted expenses	$1,200,500	$1,200,500	$0
TOTAL ACTIVITY COSTS	$9,363,598	$9,530,532	($166,934)

40 FTEs and a 20% allowance. That's it. Now we just need to go to the incremental analysis on Schedule IA-01 and see the change in activity cost."

"So," Jim continued, "you can see an estimated savings of $167,000 at our current level of operations if we were able to reduce the indirect activity allowance to 10%. You can also see where the savings come from."

"That was quick and easy," said Marcella. "And as I look at where the savings come from and their magnitude, they all

INCREMENTAL ANALYSIS			Schedule IA-01
PlumbCo, Inc.		10:34 AM	5-Jan-20
	Total Activity Costs		Increase
	After	Before	(Decrease)
SALARIES AND WAGES			
Salaries	$2,150,720	$2,150,720	$0
Hourly	$2,709,253	$2,709,253	$0
Paid time-off benefits	$269,109	$269,108	$0
Overtime shift premium & special comp.	$122,842	$122,842	$0
TOTAL SALARIES & WAGES	$5,251,923	$5,251,923	$0
FRINGE BENEFITS			
Purchased Benefits and Taxes	$1,729,530	$1,729,530	$0
OPERATING EXPENSES			
Capital Preservation Allowance	$236,307	$297,500	($61,193)
Cost of capital	$0	$0	$0
Leases and rentals	$0	$26,000	($26,000)
Utilities	$238,679	$238,679	$0
Purch maint. & supplies	$466,400	$466,400	$0
Administrative supplies	$320,000	$320,000	$0
Other fixed and budgeted expenses	$1,200,500	$1,200,500	$0
TOTAL ACTIVITY COSTS	$9,443,339	$9,530,532	($87,193)

pass the smell test. I like it. What happens if we use the capital preservation allowance instead of depreciation?"

"That's even easier," replied Jim. "I'll start with the original model, go to the very top, and enter the number '1' in the cell in front of the instruction to 'enter 1 to activate the capital preservation allowance.' That's it. Now we can check the IA-01 schedule." He scrolled down to the schedule.

"So," said Marcella, "it reduces the cost by $87,000. How come the lease cost goes away?"

"The lease cost is included in the capital preservation allowance. If we left it in the 'after' numbers, it would be in there twice."

"What impact does replacing depreciation with the allowance have on the equipment rates?"

Jim went back to the keyboard. "First I'll turn the CPA switch back to '0' to give us the rates with deprecation. The rates are shown on Schedule RC-01."

Shearing		$44,062	3,300	Equip Hours	$13.352
Press < 75T		$429,863	10,300	Equip Hours	$41.734
Press 75T-125T		$411,900	6,000	Equip Hours	$68.650
Press > 125T		$539,561	7,800	Equip Hours	$69.715
Packaging		$210,256	11,200	Equip Hours	$18.773

"Then I'll turn the switch back on."

Shearing		$41,298	3,300	Equip Hours	$12.515
Press < 75T		$426,502	10,300	Equip Hours	$41.408
Press 75T-125T		$375,372	6,000	Equip Hours	$62.562
Press > 125T		$532,738	7,800	Equip Hours	$68.300
Packaging		$207,565	11,200	Equip Hours	$18.533

"You can see the biggest impact is on the mid-sized presses. The rate drops almost 10% using the capital preservation allowance."

"That does make sense," said Marcella. "The newest presses are in the 75-ton to 125-ton category, and those are the presses with the lowest uptime percentage. Those two factors would combine to make the rate too high using depreciation expense."

"Yeah, it looks like the capital preservation allowance is doing its job."

"Try this for me: What if we double the uptime of the mid-sized presses? Make it 12,000 hours instead of 6,000. That would make all of our equipment close to practical capacity."

"Okay," said Jim, "I'll double the mid-sized press hours on Schedule RI-01. That will impact the amount of production labor we'll need, so I'll check the bottom of schedule RI-04. You can see that without additional FTEs, we'd need to run over 22% overtime, which is far above our overtime target. If I raise the headcount from 40 to 46, the overtime will be back in the acceptable range: a little over 6%. Now we can check the results."

"First, let's look at the incremental impact on Schedule IA-01. The increase in salaries and wages makes sense. If you take 6,000 more uptime hours on the mid-sized presses and multiply by the crew size of 1.5, you'll get 9,000 labor hours. Add in the 20% indirect activity allowance, and you'll be at 10,800 hours.

INCREMENTAL ANALYSIS   Schedule IA-01
PlumbCo, Inc.   11:22 AM   5-Jan-20

| | Total Activity Costs | | Increase |
	After	Before	(Decrease)
SALARIES AND WAGES			
Salaries	$2,150,720	$2,150,720	$0
Hourly	$2,882,053	$2,709,253	$172,800
Paid time-off benefits	$287,924	$269,108	$18,816
Overtime shift premium & special comp.	$121,704	$122,842	($1,138)
TOTAL SALARY & WAGES	$5,442,401	$5,251,923	$190,478
FRINGE BENEFITS			
Purchased Benefits and Taxes	$1,811,181	$1,729,530	$81,650
OPERATING EXPENSES			
Capital Preservation Allowance	$256,287	$236,307	$19,980
Cost of capital	$0	$0	$0
Leases and rentals	$0	$0	$0
Utilities	$283,319	$238,679	$44,640
Purch maint. & supplies	$559,400	$466,400	$93,000
Administrative supplies	$320,600	$320,000	$600
Other fixed and budgeted expenses	$1,200,500	$1,200,500	$0
TOTAL ACTIVITY COSTS	$9,873,688	$9,443,339	$430,349

Multiply 10,800 hours by the production labor wage rate of $16, and that's $172,800.

"The purchased benefits and taxes make sense as well. There are three headcount-driven items in this category: health insurance and federal and state unemployment taxes. Those total $9,275 per person. The payroll dollar-driven items are FICA, Medicare, workers' compensation, and retirement contributions. They total 13.65% of payroll dollars. If you take the $190,478 increase in payroll dollars, multiply it by 13.65%, and add it to the product of six additional heads, then multiply that by $9,275 per head, you arrive at $81,650.

"As for operating costs, the CPA, utility, and purchased maintenance/supplies, 'per-hour' costs for mid-sized presses are $3.33, $7.44, and $15.50, respectively. Multiply each of those by 6,000 hours, and you arrive at the amounts on the incremental analysis. Finally, administrative supplies for production workers is at $100 each, so the six additional workers increase that cost by $600."

"What about the change in the hourly cost of a mid-sized press?" asked Marcella.

"Let's see." Jim looked at his notes from the previous run of the model. "At 6,000 hours of uptime and with the capital preservation allowance, the rate was $62.56 per hour. After increasing the uptime hours to 12,000, it's down to $48.53."

"Fourteen dollars. That's quite a drop. Are you sure that's right?"

Jim looked at some of the model details and said, "There were $217,000 of fixed costs assigned to the mid-sized presses in the 6,000-hour scenario. That's about $36 per hour. In the 12,000-hour scenario, there are $267,000 of fixed costs."

"Wait a minute," interrupted Marcella. "How can the fixed costs go up? Aren't they fixed?"

"They're fixed as far as the company goes," answered Jim, "but some of them are distributed to specific activities based on uptime, so the distribution will vary when uptime changes. That's the case here. We've taken the costs of Quality Control and Material Handling and distributed them among the five production activities based on uptime. The costs of Quality Control and Material Handling remained fixed, but more was assigned to mid-sized presses because of their increased uptime."

"I thought maybe I caught you there. Continue ..."

"Okay. The $267,000 of fixed costs works out to about $22 per hour. Hence, our $14-per-hour drop in the press rate."

"You've got this thing down, don't you?" declared Marcella.

"I've been living with this model since about Christmas. That's nearly six months. I ought to know it inside and out."

"It appears that you do."

"Let's try this ..."

Marcella and Jim went on to play with their new toy until 7:00 that evening. Marcella challenged Jim to simulate every type of decision situation she could think of, and in each case the model arrived at a financially logical and explainable answer. She couldn't wait to share the new model with Alex and the rest of PlumbCo's management.

Chapter 39

"Hey, Marcella!" It was Chris Scheele standing in Marcella's doorway.

"Oh, hi, Chris. What's up?"

"When you've got a few minutes, I'd like to go over an idea I've come up with about measuring manufacturing efficiency."

"Give me a half hour," she replied. "Your space or mine?"

"Come on over to my office. We can look at an example I've got on my computer."

"Sounds good. Be there shortly."

A half hour later, Marcella arrived at Chris' office. He motioned her to sit on his side of the desk so she could see his computer screen.

"So what's this new idea?" she asked.

"I was thinking of the more granular information we're now collecting to support our new costing model, and I thought we might be able to put some of it to use in creating a few new manufacturing metrics."

Somehow, this didn't surprise Marcella. The more she worked with Chris, the more impressed she was with his ability to turn abstract concepts into mathematical models.

"Up until now, we've only measured manufacturing as a single activity. Production labor was a single pool of costs as was manufacturing overhead. We had standards for labor so that at the end of any accounting period, we could compare actual production labor to standard production labor and arrive at an overall labor efficiency percentage. For example, if we incurred 6,354 actual labor hours, but earned only 5,120 hours, we'd say our efficiency was 78.4%. That was about it. It was a metric, but it was not a very useful one.

"Now, however, we're collecting a lot more manufacturing data in more detail. In particular, we're collecting equipment uptime and production labor by our five different manufacturing activities. In addition, our routings are now described in terms of equipment time required. Standard labor is derived from those uptime numbers using each activity's standard crew size. This provides a lot more raw data that we can use to evaluate manufacturing performance in more detail."

"I hadn't thought about that," said Marcella. "I've been thinking only in terms of developing cost information to support decisions, but this does open up new possibilities for creating performance measures. What have you got?"

"Our new focus on uptime suggested to me that not all of what we call 'labor efficiency' is actually labor efficiency. There's *equipment efficiency* as well. Some of what we describe as labor's inefficiency is caused by the equipment taking more time to produce the product. Although some of that excess time might be caused by the production workers, production labor could also be 100% efficient while the equipment is running. The equipment is just taking longer than expected to make the product. So I thought it might be informative to separate equipment efficiency from labor efficiency. I've got a worksheet here on my screen with an example of what I think we could do. At this point, the numbers in the worksheet are fictitious, but I think they're fairly realistic.

"Before our cost model changes, all we would report would be the number in the upper left-hand corner of the schedule. We show the 78.4% overall efficiency."

Marcella laughed. "That's where you got the rather precise actual and standard hours you mentioned earlier."

"Yeah. That's where I got them. Now we could simply do the same calculation, but for each of the five activity centers. That's what I thought of first and show at the top of the schedule. We'd be able to zero in on the efficiency of each individual activity. We'd be better able to focus our attention on areas where the problems were more pronounced."

	Total	Shearing	Press < 75T	Press 75T-125T	Press > 125T	Packaging
Actual Labor Hours	6,534	638	1,575	1,024	1,113	2,185
Standard Labor Hours	5,120	480	1,200	675	915	1,850
Production Labor Efficiency	**78.4%**	**75.2%**	**76.2%**	**65.9%**	**82.2%**	**84.7%**

	Total	Shearing	Press < 75T	Press 75T-125T	Press > 125T	Packaging
Actual Equipment Hours	3,250	290	840	525	645	950
Actual Labor Hours	6,534	638	1,575	1,024	1,113	2,185
Activity Capacity Hours (80 hours/week)	5,376	336	1,344	1,680	1,008	1,008
Capacity Utilization	**60.5%**	**86.3%**	**62.5%**	**31.3%**	**64.0%**	**94.2%**
Standard Equipment Hours	3,025	240	800	450	610	925
Equipment Efficiency	**93.1%**	**82.8%**	**95.2%**	**85.7%**	**94.6%**	**97.4%**
Standard Crew Size		2.0	1.5	1.5	1.5	2.0
Standard Labor @ Actual Equipment Hours	5,495	580	1,260	788	968	1,900

	Total	Shearing	Press < 75T	Press 75T-125T	Press > 125T	Packaging
Labor Efficiency	84.1%	90.9%	80.0%	76.9%	87.0%	87.0%
Standard Equipment Hours		240	800	450	610	925
Standard Crew Size		2.0	1.5	1.5	1.5	2.0
Standard Labor Hours	5,120	480	1,200	675	915	1,850
Combined Efficiency	78.4%	75.2%	76.2%	65.9%	82.2%	84.7%

"But then I started thinking about the uptime information we'll now be collecting by activity center. I thought it might provide some useful insight if we compared actual and standard uptime hours. At the same time, I thought tracking our capacity utilization would also be insightful. It's not something we paid much attention to in the past, but it does have an impact on our return on investment."

"Those both sound like worthwhile things to track," interjected Marcella. "Getting a measure of the cost of capital into the model is something Jim and have I talked about, but we've decided to put that off until we've mastered the current changes."

"The first measurement on my schedule is capacity utilization. We'll have to figure out what number we want to use as capacity, but for the example, I assumed it was 80 hours per week per machine. I'm not married to that number; I just needed a number for the schedule. Anyway, comparing the actual equipment hours to the capacity hours provides us with a capacity utilization percentage. This is something we could track over time and better manage our capital equipment.

"The second measurement takes the equipment hours earned for each activity center and matches them against the actual equipment hours. This results in what I termed *equipment efficiency*. It tells us how well the equipment performed against standard."

"What would cause equipment inefficiency?" asked Marcella.

"A lot of different things," replied Chris. "We might have noticed a problem and increased the cycle time to compensate. The equipment could have required some minor maintenance, cleaning, or adjustment during a production run. In none of those three cases would the crew be reassigned elsewhere or the equipment cease charging time to the job being run. Or the equipment could simply be waiting for material. Stuff happens.

"The third measurement takes the actual equipment uptime and multiplies by the standard crew size to arrive at the hours to compare against actual labor. That's what I termed *labor efficiency*. I think it's pretty much the same thing as your model's 'indirect activity allowance.' Again, there are a lot of possible causes. Actual crew sizes are not always the same as the standard crew sizes. If, for some reason, the workers at a machine can't keep up with the machine's rate, we'll add another person to the crew. At times, a worker can't split time between two presses, so we have four people working two presses instead of three people working them. Although we try to avoid it, we do schedule more production workers than we need to make sure a blip in absenteeism doesn't mean we can't run some of the equipment that day. And you also have trainees who are accounted for as production workers, but are not included in standard crew sizes."

Marcella was impressed. "That's an awful lot of new information you can glean from the data that will now be available."

"I must admit, it will focus my attention better. As they say, *what gets measured, gets done.* Having to report against these numbers regularly will keep me on my toes a bit more."

"Not everyone will voluntarily create more detailed performance measures against which their performance will be evaluated."

"It'll help me do a better job. That's the important thing. If I do a better job, the measures will highlight that fact. If I don't, they'll highlight that as well."

Marcella thought to herself, *This guy is exceptional.*

Chapter 40

It had been 18 months since Alex first brought up the topic of cost models with Marcella. Since that conversation, she had learned a great deal about managerial costing, expanded her understanding of PlumbCo's various operations and how they work together, gained insight into how other executives actually view accountants, and lost any confidence she had in using GAAP-based information to support business decisions. She had also managed to facilitate the company's management through the creation of a causality-based cost model that took into account the concerns of all key managers, and she had gained their support—at least in concept.

The process hadn't been smooth. It hadn't been a project that was planned out in advance. It had been more an evolutionary process as might have been expected when no one involved had done such a thing before and they were all feeling their way through uncharted territory. As is the case with any business the size of PlumbCo, the luxury of pulling people off their day-to-day jobs and assigning them to a special project was not an option. Marcella and PlumbCo's key executives and managers had to find the time in their already busy schedules to do their parts and make their contributions.

Finally, after 18 months of on-and-off work, they had what Marcella considered to be a "conceptually valid" predictive cost model—based on causality—that had been populated and calibrated with actual data from the 12-month period ended in June. It was now time to present the results to her boss and her peers. They had already agreed to the concepts in the model. She was anxious to see if they changed their tune once they saw "the numbers."

Gathered in the conference room were Alex Johnson, Chris Scheele, Rich Vivian, and Kelsey Hayes. Jim Stinson was there to provide Marcella with any backup she might need, but the meeting was hers to lead.

"You're probably wondering why I've invited you all here," said Marcella with a smile. "I'm here to prove that one of you is the murderer."

Everyone laughed. It was a good sign. Eighteen months ago, she wouldn't have had the confidence to start an important business meeting with a joke. She now viewed those in the room as her colleagues, not just co-workers, and from their response, she felt that they viewed her the same way.

"All seriousness aside," she continued, "we're here to review the results of our new cost model and to discuss possible ways we can take advantage of the information it provides." She put her first slide on the screen.

"This first slide is a summary of the costing rates generated by populating the cost model with data from the 12 months ended in June. We'll drill down on each one of these, but first take a few minutes to review the summary to see if anything jumps out at you as unusual or doesn't make sense at this high level."

"Right off," said Chris, "I'm surprised at that 43% rate we'll need to add to mold cost. I knew there was 'overhead' related to them, but I hadn't expected it to be that high."

"We'll look at the details later on," replied Marcella, "but I know there was a lot of engineering time dedicated to supporting molds. I believe that's most of the $151,000."

Activity Center	Activity Cost	Base Measure	Description	Rate
Rubber	$460,310	1,000,000	Pounds	$0.460
Purch Comps	$358,397	$2,000,000	Purchase $	17.9%
Pkg Material	$144,747	$1,000,000	Purchase $	14.5%
Molds	$151,813	$350,000	Purchase $	43.4%
Prod Labor	$2,307,688	65,150,	Labor Hours	$35.42
Press Set-Ups	$654,239	6,920	60-Minute	$42.70
		5,600	90-Minute	$64.06
Shearing	$44,062	3,300	Equip Hours	$13.35
Press < 75T	$429,863	$10,300	Equip Hours	$41.73
Press 75T-125T	$411,900	6,000	Equip Hours	$68.65
Press > 125T	$539,561	7,800	Equip Hours	$69.17
Packaging	$210,256	11,200	Equip Hours	$18.77
Put-Away	$275,149	1,200,000	Units	$0.23
Storage	$198,725	720,000	Group A	$0.06
		360,000	Group B	$0.22
		120,000	Group C	$0.66
Order Process	$305,191	1,653	Telephone	$59.07
		3,307	Mail/Fax	$29.53
		7,440	Electronic	$14.77
Order Picking	$328,280	77,040	Group A	$2.32
		32,528	Group B	$2.89
		15,408	Group C	$3.62

Activity Center	Activity Cost	Base Measure	Base Description	Rate
Shipping	$472,385	10,500	Loose Box	$11.20
		31,000	Full Box	$7.47
		5,500	Pallet	$22.41
Return/Restock	$96,246	1,250	Returns	$77.00
Box Stores	$296,726	$2,586,084	Internal Costs	11.5%
Major Retailers	$296,726	$3,694,406	Internal Costs	8.0%
Small Accounts	$347,549	$1,108,322	Internal Costs	31.4%
Growth Costs	$18,721	$8,329,813	Internal Costs	0.2%
Gen & Admin	$1,181,997	$8,348,535	Internal Costs	14.2%
Total Activity Costs	$9,530,532			

"It'll be interesting to see why the rate for the mid-sized presses is almost the same as the rate for the larger presses," noted Alex. "You'd expect it to be somewhere in between the small and large press rates."

"Two things strike me right off," added Rich, "the 66 cents per unit for storing those slow-moving Group C parts and the $77 it costs to handle a return. That's almost a hundred grand we spend to handle those things."

Kelsey looked a bit perplexed.

"What about you, Kelsey?" asked Marcella. "Anything strike you?"

"From this," she said, "it's looking like we ought to get rid of our small accounts. They're responsible for the bulk of those $59 telephone orders, and their customer support cost rate is three to four times that of the larger accounts."

Marcella was pleased that the summary had generated at least one question in each person's mind. That meant that they were at least paying attention.

	DIRECT/VALUE-ADDING ACTIVITIES						
	Shearing	Press < 75T	Press 75T-125T	Press > 125T	Packaging	Total	%
Capital Preservation Allowance	$2,211	$20,600	$19,980	$39,000	$16,016	$97,807	41.4%
Utilities	$5,115	$63,860	$44,640	$67,704	$17,360	$198,679	83.2%
Purch maint. & supplies	$6,600	$123,600	$93,000	$156,000	$67,200	$446,400	95.7%
Maintenance	$14,264	$57,057	$71,321	$85,585	$28,528	$256,755	90.0%
Bldg & Grounds	$4,479	$17,916	$32,249	$26,336	$13,437	$94,417	30.1%
Engineering	$0	$35,737	$35,737	$35,737	$35,737	$142,949	20.0%
EquipHrSupt	$8,629	$107,732	$78,445	$122,375	$29,286	$346,467	100.0%
Total	$41,298	$426,502	$375,372	$532,738	$207,565	$1,583,474	
Base	3,300	10,300	6,000	7,800	11,200		
Rate	$12.51	$41.41	$62.56	$68.30	$18.53		
	$ Equip Hour	$ Equip Hour	$ Equip Hour	$ Equip Hour	$ Equip Hour		
Rates with Depreciation Expense	$13.35	$41.73	$68.65	$69.17	$18.77		

"Now that you've put your toe in the water, let's jump in and dig into the details, give them a good smell test, discuss what they mean, and start thinking about what actions they might suggest. I'll start with the details of our manufacturing rates.

"First, let me explain how to read the slide. You can see the five manufacturing activities in the labeled columns along with a total of each element of cost assigned to these five activities in the second-to-last column. The costs directly assigned to the activities are in the first tier of costs. They're above the blank line. Below the blank line, in the second tier of costs, are those that have been distributed to these activities by support activities.

The final column—the one with the percentages—indicates the percentage of either the total cost or total support activity cost that has been assigned to manufacturing activities. With a little 'eyeball math,' you can figure out what percentage was assigned to each activity.

"For example, 83% of utilities was assigned to these five activities. With a little 'eyeball math,' you can determine that the $44,000 assigned to 75-ton to 125-ton presses represents about 22% of that 83%, or 18% of the total."

"You may be overestimating our mathematical abilities," laughed Kelsey.

"Perhaps," said Marcella, "but I did it this way for two reasons. First, we'd be looking at slides all day if I did each activity one-by-one. Second, I thought it would be more meaningful if you could see the numbers relative to one another as well as to their base. Still looking at utilities, you can see that very little is assigned to Shearing or Packaging while quite a bit is assigned to the presses. That ought to make sense. You can also see by dividing the utility cost by the base—which is uptime hours—that the under-75-ton activity gets about $6 per hour, the 75-125-ton category gets about $7.50 per hour, and the large presses get closer to $9 per hour. I hope this makes sense to you."

"I like it," interjected Alex. "You can also break down the rate into its components. For example, I can see that the $12 of the $41 rate for small presses is for purchased maintenance and supplies, and about $10 of it is that EquipHrSupt item. By the way, what is *EquipHrSupt*?"

"That stands for 'equipment hour support.' It's basically the inspection work done by Quality Control and in-process material movement done by Material Handling. We figured those two activities would follow 'the action' in the plant. The more equipment hours there were, the more inspection and material handling there would be. We didn't treat all the hours equally, however. For example, an hour in Shearing was weighted only about one-fifth as heavily as an hour in the mid-sized presses. Similarly, an hour of the large press time was weighted 50% higher than an hour of small press time. We figured that would take care of the differences due to the size of the parts and amount of inspection required."

"Understood," replied Alex.

"I also included what the rate would be if we included depreciation expense instead of the capital preservation allowance at the bottom of the schedule," added Marcella.

"It looks like the only one where it made much of a difference was in the mid-sized presses," said Rich. "Why do you think that is?"

Chris pitched in, "It's probably because we have several newer presses there and the fact that we probably have too many of them."

"Too many?" asked Alex.

"Yeah," replied Chris. "We've got five presses, and we ran only 6,000 hours during the 12-month period. That's only 1,200 hours each. Unless we feel we're going to need the extra capacity in the future, we could probably get rid of two of the older ones, generate a little cash, and maybe reduce our maintenance cost. It would also provide some open floor space for future expansion."

"Let's look into that," replied Alex. "Okay, carry on, Marcella."

"The next slide shows a summary of our six warehousing activities. It's set up the same way as the previous slide."

	Put-Away	Storage	Order Process	Order Picking	Shipping	Return/ Restock	Total	%
			EVENT AND TRANSACTION ACTIVITIES					
Other fixed and budgeted expenses	0%	0%	0%	0%	$200,000	$0	$200,000	16.7%
Bldg & Grounds	$3,583	$143,327	$0	$0	$8,958	$0	$155,868	49.7%
Acct & Finance	$0	$0	$71,225	$0	$0	$0	$71,225	10.0%
Cust Service	$0	$0	$233,463	$0	$0	$12,288	$245,750	100.0%
Quality Control	$0	$0	$0	$0	$0	$26,569	$26,569	5.0%
Mat'l Handling	$161,558	$32,312	$0	$0	$0	$16,156	$210,026	65.0%
Ship & Receive	$0	$0	$0	$0	$179,909	$13,839	$193,748	70.0%
Whse Labor	$109,418	xxxxxx	xxxxxx	$328,254	$82,064	$27,355	$547,090	100.0%
Total	$274,559	$175,639	$304,687	$328,254	$470,930	$96,206	$1,650,276	
Base Rate	See Weighted Rate Schedule	See Weighted Rate Schedule	See Weighted Rate Schedule	See Weighted Rate Schedule	See Weighted Rate Schedule	See Weighted Rate Schedule		

"What makes up that fixed and budgeted expense in Shipping?" asked Rich.

"Mostly miscellaneous packaging materials and transportation costs. Stuff that's not big enough to link to specific customers, but does relate to shipping activities. I'd like to have gotten more specific with it, but I didn't think it would be worth the effort—at least, not at this point. You're always welcome to dig deeper into it for a future iteration of the model."

"I think I'll put it on my to-do list," said Rich. "I can also see why returns cost so much. Just about everybody appears to get involved when product comes back. It doesn't look like it takes a lot of anyone's time, it just takes a little of a lot of people's time. Maybe we should pay more attention as to why goods are returned, and see what we can do to get that number down."

"I suspect," added Kelsey, "we've got some customers that you might call 'return addicts.' It would be interesting to see who they are."

"We'll see that when we do our customer profitability analyses with these rates. The return costs will be assigned to those customers making the returns. That should give us some insight into whether some customers abuse our fairly easy return policy."

"I'm curious," said Alex, "about the warehousing labor attached to putting parts away in the warehouse. Isn't that the job of the material handlers who take them over from manufacturing? The warehousing labor for put-away is around 40% of the cost of putting the parts in their assigned warehouse location."

Rich clarified the process. "The material handlers deliver the parts to their location, but the warehousing folks help them load them into their cubes, make sure the parts are organized for efficient picking, and do cycle counts to make sure the perpetual inventory balances are correct." He thought for a moment and added, "Some of those warehousing labor activities might have belonged in Storage and not in Put-Away."

"That's easily corrected," said Marcella. "Any other observations or questions?"

The meeting went on for another two hours. The session resulted in no major changes to the model. It did, however, evoke a lot of discussion as to what the information meant and how it could be exploited. By meeting's end, Alex had tasked each manager with developing a list of possible ways their area of responsibility might be able to use this new cost data to improve PlumbCo's long-term financial performance.

As the meeting broke up, Jim—who had only been called upon to support 'the numbers' a couple of times—looked at Marcella and said, "I think you nailed it, boss."

"You mean *we* nailed it," she answered. "You, the Major, and me. I was just the mouthpiece this morning. This was the culmination of the Major's subtle—and sometimes not-so-subtle—hints and suggestions, your imagination and hard work, and my having the sense to pay attention to the two of you. I think I owe you lunch. Where would you like to go?"

They both laughed as they headed to the parking lot.

Chapter 41

Ten days after the group meeting to discuss the model's results, Marcella met with Kelsey Hayes to talk about possible actions suggested by the new cost information that could improve customer profitability. After exchanging pleasantries and engaging in a few minutes of small talk, Marcella got to the topic at hand.

"Well, Kelsey, have you given any more thought to the discussions we had during our meeting to go over the model?"

"As a matter of fact," she answered, "I have. It helped that you and I threw around some ideas and then went over some of the preliminary numbers with Jim earlier. It provided my brain with a little 'spring training' before hitting the regular season with the real numbers from our last meeting. Prior to this project, I had never given any thought to how our customers behave. My concern was to get them to buy the stuff. To me, a sale was a sale. How much profit we made on the sale was somebody else's concern. Now I realize that a customer's ordering behavior can have a pretty significant impact on their profitability.

"So," she continued, "I think I need to somehow get their ordering behavior incorporated into the formula we use to establish their discounts from list price and then get the agreed-to behavior included as part of our sales contract with each customer. That way, if they vary from the agreed-to behavior, the discount can be rescinded, or at least modified."

"That sounds like a good approach," replied Marcella. "Would we do that only with new contracts, or could we do it on existing contracts?"

"We haven't established any customary practice with new customers, so that wouldn't be a problem. It would be a bit different with existing customers. Our biggest customers are pretty much in the driver's seat, and we wouldn't want to put their business at risk by reducing their discounts if their behavior is a bit costly. As the accounts get smaller, however, I think it might be worth the risk of losing their business to require a change in their ordering behavior to keep their discounts."

"You know," said Marcella, "it might turn out for some of them that we could offer additional discounts if they change their behavior. If the fulfillment cost decrease is greater than the revenue decrease, it would be a win/win arrangement." Marcella thought for a few moments. "Jim will be able to provide you with a breakdown of each customer's profitability, like the ones he used as examples earlier, and you could see which customers would be good to approach with such a proposal." She then hesitated. "However, that might be pretty time-consuming to do one at a time."

"That's true. Not only to do the analyses, but to contact each one individually with a proposal. We have an awful lot of small customers."

"What if we don't address individual customers, but make some kind of blanket offer to a group of small customers that we believe can become more profitable with a change in behavior?"

"Is there a way we could do that?" Kelsey asked. "Isn't each customer's situation pretty unique? Wouldn't we risk making the profitability even worse for some of them?"

"I'm just thinking out loud here, but it seems to me that one of the biggest issues among the small customers would be with those who order often and don't order electronically. Each telephone order costs almost $60, and each mail or fax order around $30, while an electronic order costs only $15. Getting them to order electronically would, in and of itself, improve their profitability. But that's not all. If the customer's overall volume remains the same and they order less frequently, there would also be fewer line items to pick; we'd pick more items per visit to a warehouse location." Marcella paused briefly before continuing, "We might be able to identify a group of customers that place more than a certain number of orders annually either by phone, fax, or mail and offer them an additional discount if they ordered electronically once each quarter. That should reduce both their order-processing costs and order-picking costs."

"I think you've got something there. That might cover 300 or 400 customers. Do you think we could come up with an offer like that where we could be sure it wouldn't make any of them even less profitable?"

"I'm thinking that if such an offer made 90% of them more profitable and 10% somewhat less profitable, it would still be a win for us. And a group offer would require a lot less effort than dealing with each one of them individually."

"I like it," exclaimed Kelsey. "Can I steal Jim to help me figure out which customers we should include in the group and what the new discount parameters should be?"

"You don't have to steal him," laughed Marcella. "It's part of his job."

"That takes care of a lot of small existing customers, but how about our big customers and new customers? Discounts with our larger customers are usually negotiated here at the home office, but our salespeople usually need to make quick decisions while negotiating with other customers. The prospective customer wants to know right then and there what the deal would be, so our sales reps need to be authorized to make certain discount decisions on the spot. Historically, we give them authority to grant discounts of up to 5% without home-office approval if the customer's anticipated volume is above $2,000, 10% if it's above $5,000, and 15% if it's above $15,000. But it won't be as easy as that anymore. All this customer behavior information will need to be taken into account. My sales staff is made up of people with selling skills, not math skills. It might be a bit too complex for them to quickly do the math on the back of an envelope."

"Are they pretty tech savvy?" asked Marcella. "Are they comfortable using electronic devices while conversing with the customer?"

"Oh yes! I don't think any of them could live without all their electronic devices."

"Then perhaps we could create an app for them to use. They could enter best estimates of the key data into the app and have an allowable discount determined."

"What kind of key data would they need to enter?"

"Oh, like the number of different SKUs the customer anticipates buying, the annual volume of parts it's likely to buy, how the customer plans on ordering and how often, stuff like that."

Kelsey chuckled, "You know they'll always overstate everything, don't you? Our salesperson will want to make the sale, so he or she will probably bump the numbers up a bit. And our customers will want the biggest discount, so they'll most likely do the same."

"Yeah, that would be a problem," replied Marcella. "How about something like this—I'm still just thinking out loud here, I might get to the end and say 'strike that from the record.'"

"I understand," laughed Kelsey.

"We upload the information on which the customer's discount is based, and then we match that information against the customer's actual behavior. We'd give a grace period up front while enough time passes—say, 3–6 months—to give us a representative sample size. From that point on, we'd track actual vs. 'discount assumed' behavior, and we'd have the system raise some kind of red flag when actual behavior no longer generates the savings anticipated when the discount was granted. Our standard contract could be adjusted to allow us to unilaterally void the discount if the promised behavior is not observed."

"Can we do all that?" asked Kelsey.

"I'm sure there are ways to do it," answered Marcella, "but we'll have to figure out if we can find one that would be cost effective for us."

"And first we'll have to figure out what kind of parameters we'd put into the app," added Kelsey.

"I think that's something else you and Jim could work on. I'll brief him on our conversation and tell him that the two of you have been tasked with developing the basics for an app that could support our proposed new discounting policies. Once we have that, we can start on the IT folks. Do you think that's enough for one sitting?"

Kelsey grinned. "To tell the truth, I think I might have gone over my limit during this get-together. My brain is suffering a few cramps right now. Let's break if off and pick it up again after Jim and I have spent some time on our assignment."

Chapter 42

Shortly after her meeting with Kelsey Hayes, Marcella arranged to visit Chris Scheele in his office to see whether he had any new thoughts about PlumbCo's manufacturing activities after seeing the results of the cost model.

"*Bonjour, ma chère!*" said Chris as she entered.

"You've been working on your French again, eh?"

"Just a little. Enough to surprise people once in a while. I can't actually carry on a conversation in French. I just remember little tidbits and blurt them out once in a while."

"You know, Chris," said Marcella, "I think I've figured you out."

"You have? How's that?"

"You're one of those people who takes their work seriously while not taking themselves seriously. You're exceptional at what you do, yet you like to make fun of yourself and downplay your part in solving a problem or reaching a goal. You're always throwing in one-liners in the middle of serious discussions. I've seen you deliberately give someone a roundabout and confusing answer to a fairly straightforward question just to see if they'd get it."

"How'd you know that's why I gave them that kind of answer?"

"Because of the smile on your face when you gave it. Your answer wasn't intended to embarrass them, but to surprise them, lighten the atmosphere a bit, and make them think."

Chris laughed and said, "I've found that being too serious gets in the way of accomplishing what you're trying to get done. People get too uptight and stressed out. I found that a relaxed but still focused atmosphere works best for getting the job done. You don't want people to love the work but hate the job. I try to do what I can to make them love both."

"By all accounts," replied Marcella, "you've done that quite well. Anyway, on to the purpose of my visit. Did our presentation of the cost model's results stimulate your 'little gray cells' at all?"

"I don't know if 'stimulate' is the right word, but the model did highlight one item that I believe I need to address immediately and other data I can use to assess some of the ideas I've been toying with for quite some time."

"What was it that you feel needs your immediate attention?" asked Marcella.

"The 20% indirect activity allowance. Intuition tells me that some sort of indirect activity allowance is inevitable and can't be avoided. After all, you can't immediately 'beam' workers from one job to the next; there's some lost time there. And we do bring in a few more production workers than we actually need each day to make sure we can cover for absenteeism. But 20% seems awfully high to me. I'd be comfortable with 5–10% maybe, but not 20%.

"So I called Jim and asked him to use the model to give me an estimate of how much money we would save if we could reduce the indirect activity allowance from 20% to 10%. Five minutes later, he showed up at my office. I thought maybe he had a question or needed some clarification, but no, he had already completed an analysis that showed a potential $170,000 reduction in costs. I think I've got a copy of his summary right here." Chris pulled the analysis from his desk drawer.

"As he explained it, he needed to change only two numbers. He reduced the 20% indirect activity allowances to 10% and then changed the required production labor headcount to match the lower demand for production labor. Let's see," Chris looked at his notes, "lowering the percentage from 20% to 10% would result in the need for 3,643 less production labor hours. Lowering our production labor headcount by two heads would enable us to provide the required labor while working 3.5% overtime. At the 20% rate, we not only had two more workers, but worked 7.3% overtime. The net result is a projected savings of $170,847."

"Sounds like something well worth digging into," interjected Marcella.

"Definitely. We're going to start by revising our efficiency reports to the format I went over with you last month. The one where we break it down by activity center, capacity utilization, equipment efficiency, and labor efficiency. I'm hoping that helps us zero in on the areas where the problem is greatest. Once we have a handle on the 'where,' we can better begin assessing the 'why.'"

INCREMENTAL ANALYSIS   Schedule IA-01
PlumbCo, Inc.   10:59 AM   20-Jan-20

| | Total Activity Costs | | Increase |
	After	Before	(Decrease)
SALARIES AND WAGES			
Salaries	$2,150,720	$2,150,720	$0
Hourly	$2,605,013	$2,709,253	($104,240)
Paid time-off benefits	$262,836	$269,108	($6,272)
Overtime shift premium & special comp.	$99,525	$122,842	($23,317)
TOTAL SALARIES & WAGES	$5,118,094	$5,251,923	($133,829)
FRINGE BENEFITS			
Purchased Benefits and Taxes	$1,692,713	$1,729,530	($36,818)
OPERATING EXPENSES			
Depreciation	$297,500	$297,500	$0
Cost of capital	$0	$0	$0
Leases and rentals	$26,000	$26,000	$0
Utilities	$238,679	$238,679	$0
Purch maint. & supplies	$466,400	$466,400	$0
Administrative supplies	$319,800	$320,000	($200)
Other fixed and budgeted expenses	$1,200,500	$1,200,500	$0
TOTAL ACTIVITY COSTS	$9,359,685	$9,530,532	($170,847)

"Sounds like a good approach. You mentioned some other ideas. Can you share them with me? I know how to keep a secret."

"They're not secrets. They're ideas I've floated around before. I just never had any kind of numbers to measure their advisability. Now, however, we should be able to evaluate them."

"And those ideas are ...?"

"The first has to do with getting rid of one or two of our mid-sized presses. The model makes it pretty clear that we have too much capacity there. It showed that we have more than twice the capacity we currently need: something like 13,000 available press hours to meet the 6,000-hour demand. Part of my rationale relates to the discussion we had about the overall objective of the company: profit as a percentage of sales versus return on investment. Those excess press hours represent an investment on which we're not getting any return. Maybe we could turn that dead investment into something that will generate a return."

"Do you think we could get much if we sold two of the presses?" asked Marcella.

"Oh, my best guess is that we'd be able to get $50,000 or $60,000 out of it. I haven't done any research yet; that's just a guess based on past experience."

"Are you sure we're not going to need those hours in the future?"

"Not in the next four or five years anyway," Chris replied. "As a matter of fact, I'm not too sure how we came to have such a surplus of those presses. Jake must have overestimated the demand going forward. He pretty much determined where we spent our capital money without a lot of input from anyone else. I sure don't see it."

"Is there anything you think would be a good alternative use for the $50–$60,000 we might realize by selling the presses?"

"Right now, there's nothing on my 'need-to-have' shopping list for manufacturing. But there might be some good uses for the funds in Rich's arena. Or in the link between his arena and mine. Rich has been lobbying for more investment to support distribution for years, but Jake's focus was always on manufacturing when it came to capital spending. He didn't think that much in terms of distribution. I think this costing project and the information developed in the model has changed everyone's perspective. Even as a manufacturing guy, I can see the importance of effective distribution on our profitability. Rich's needs probably deserve more attention than they've gotten in the past."

"I'll make sure to find out what he thinks he needs when I talk with him," replied Marcella.

"Make sure you've got a lot of time," laughed Chris. "He's got a lot of ideas that no one has paid much attention to over the years. He may try to lay them all on you at once."

"I'll keep that in mind," replied Marcella. "You mentioned you had ideas, plural. Care to share another?"

"Sure. I'll be curious as to the actual cost of producing some of our lowest-volume and slowest-moving products. Our set-up costs aren't major, but some of the parts' volumes are awfully small. I've often wondered whether we might be better off if we found some other, smaller company to produce some, if not most, of those items."

"What would that do for us?" asked Marcella.

"Possibly nothing in the short term. Maybe it would even increase our out-of-pocket costs a bit. But from a long-term perspective, our ability to grow without adding more capacity would be improved. See, Keeper of the Privy Purse, you've succeeded in getting me to think in terms of long-term return on investment, not short-term profit. If we can structure the arrangements with a supplier right, we might also be able to tie up less money in inventory for shorter periods of time. Thus far it's only been a thought, but I figure that, at some point, Jim and I would be able to use the new model to run a few possible scenarios to see what the impact might be."

"That would be a great exercise and good use of the model."

"I thought it might. But right now, it's just an idea. I don't plan on mentioning it to anyone else until we've run some numbers."

"What idea?" laughed Marcella. "See, I told you I can keep a secret."

Chapter 43

"You know," said Rich Vivian, "now that we've gone through the process of creating a cost model of the warehouse and populating it with some real numbers, my brain takes me in a different direction every time I walk out onto the warehouse floor."

"How's that?" asked Marcella with a grin. "Do you physically walk off in a different direction?"

"No, but watching my folks work triggers different types of thoughts than it did before. My mind now hangs a cost on the things they do, something it never did before. I used to think about how we could do things more efficiently, but there was no cost attached to that efficiency. After all, we're a warehouse. There's no way to cost the things you do in a warehouse—or at least that's what I thought. Now when someone is preparing a loose box for shipment, I think about the $11 it's costing. Or when someone is headed to pick a slow-moving item, I think about the $3.60 that's costing. That's the different direction my mind now goes."

"Is that good or bad? Does it make you uncomfortable?"

"Oh! It's definitely a change for the better. I'm just a bit surprised at how much differently I look at things now. This stuff we're doing in the warehouse is measurable, and we're measuring it. I've got fairly detailed measurables that I can try to improve on."

"Have you seen any particular areas you think you'd be able to improve on?" asked Marcella.

"One of the things that struck me when you presented the model was the cost of putting things away in the warehouse. It was around $275,000, which seemed like an awful lot of money. When Jim showed me what went into that number, I was surprised that about 20% of my crew's work was involved. I had thought it was a lot less—more like 5%. I guess I just didn't realize that's what they were doing. I think a lot of it isn't really put-away but 'tidying up' and reorganizing parts that are already there."

Rich continued, "But that accounts for only 40% of the cost; the rest comes from manufacturing's material handlers delivering the parts to the warehouse. From what Jim tells me, almost half of material handling's effort related to moving parts from manufacturing to the warehouse. Half of what they do! That doesn't seem reasonable. I followed up with Chris, and the two of us found that there is an awful lot of handling between the time a part is complete in its package and it is delivered to the warehouse. It's sometimes moved three or four times."

"That would explain why the amount of material handling is so high. You'd think it would need to be handled only once or twice," interjected Marcella.

"Yeah! That's what I thought. I guess it's got something to do with their trying to organize things for orderly delivery to the warehouse. I'm not too sure what that means."

"Did Chris say anything about it?"

Rich laughed. "He said that you'd probably get on us for not having a good handle on the activities that connect us. I think he was joking."

"I'd never 'get on' you guys,'" replied Marcella. "I'm just as guilty as anyone else because the cost information the system generated just buried the cost of those activities in overhead. That made them pretty much invisible."

"Chris did suggest that I see if there is any capital investment we could make to streamline the movement of product between us." Rich hesitated for a moment before asking, "Do you think PlumbCo would consider spending capital money on the warehouse?"

"I don't see why not."

"The company hasn't been too keen on doing it in the past. Just about every idea I've had has gotten shot down, and the available capital has been directed toward manufacturing."

"Well," said Marcella, "now we have measurables that we can use to determine the financial benefit of any proposed capital project you might suggest. If the potential benefit is sufficient and funds are available, I don't see why it being a warehousing project and not a manufacturing project would be a factor."

"Forgive me if I don't really believe that until I see it," replied Rich.

"You're forgiven, and your doubt is understandable. But if you find a solution and it needs capital funds to get done, either Jim or I should be able to use the model to estimate the benefit and come up with a return on investment for the project. If it looks good, you'll have my backing. By the way, I think you'll have Chris' backing as well. He mentioned that you guys had been shorted on capital over the years and probably deserve a little more attention."

"Really! Chris said that?"

"Something to that effect. Are there any other things you'd like to pursue other than reducing the put-away cost?"

"Remember our discussions about cubes?" asked Rich.

"Sure," replied Marcella. "Each part number has its own cube and they're organized in the warehouse based on the part's popularity."

"That's right. But all the cubes are the same size, and for some of the low-volume, slow-moving parts—you know, the FISH inventory—the cubes are mostly filled with air. Going back to our conversation awhile back about the parts 'renting' space in the warehouse, these parts need a one-bedroom apartment, but we're renting them a five-bedroom townhouse. I was thinking it might be more effective if we divide some of the five-bedroom units into multiple one-bedroom units and assign the FISH inventory there. That would make better use of our available warehouse space and reduce the cost per part for storage."

"That looks like it's worth pursuing. And it doesn't need any capital. Would it disrupt your operation while you move things around and update the inventory and picking software for the changes?"

"I don't think so, but I'll talk to my people and the IT folks before doing anything."

"Have you spoken to Kelsey about any of the steps she'll be taking?"

"Not recently."

"Check in with her when you get a chance. She's going to try to induce our smaller customers to order electronically and less frequently by using bigger discounts as an incentive. The electronic orders won't affect you much. That'll lighten the load in customer service. But the 'less frequently' should mean that you'll have fewer line items to pick. If a customer orders quarterly instead of monthly, the line items to support that customer should drop by two-thirds or so."

"That would be great," said Rich. "It ought to save us some money."

"Based on the model," responded Marcella, "a 10% reduction in line items would drop the headcount required by four-tenths of a head. So unless we reduce total line items by around 20%–25%, we probably wouldn't be able to reduce the number of people in the warehouse. However, we are planning on growing, and it would enable us to pick a lot more parts with the same number of people doing the picking. That would be the long-term benefit."

"Let's hope she's successful."

"How about shipments?" asked Marcella.

"What about shipments?" replied Rich.

"We spend close to $500,000 on shipments. Have you had time to give any thought to how we might improve there?"

"To be honest with you, no. I guess I've been thinking about this sequentially. First parts arrive and are put away. Then they are stored. Then they are picked. My brain hasn't gotten around to shipping yet."

"That's fine." Marcella gave Rich a reassuring smile. "You can't do everything at once. I was just curious. Now that all these activities that were once submerged in a sea of overhead have now surfaced as measurable work activities, they raise a lot of questions, don't they?"

"Yeah. You're right. As I said before, my brain now takes me in a different direction every time I walk out onto the warehouse floor."

Chapter 44

"Did you have many kids stop by last night?" asked Alex as he settled himself into one of Marcella's visitor chairs. "We only had about 50, but we live in a pretty mature neighborhood. There aren't a lot of young families living there anymore."

"Oh, we had the normal Halloween at our place," replied Marcella. "About 200 kids. Paul always makes sure we prepare for about 300 … and he makes sure we hand out Butterfingers last. Those are his favorite, and it's his annual excuse for eating excessive amounts of candy 'just to get them out of the way.'"

"I'm rather partial to Butterfingers myself," laughed Alex. "That's why we don't buy them to pass out. I'd eat all the leftovers."

After a five-minute discussion about the pros and cons of various Halloween handouts, Alex finally got around to the point of his visit.

"I understand you had a chance to meet with each of your peers to discuss the results of the cost model, one on one. How'd it go?"

"I thought they all went great. Kelsey was first, and she seemed quite interested in exploring the possibility of enticing many of our smaller customers into ordering larger quantities less often and doing it electronically with some special discounts. She was also interested in coming up with a tool her salespeople could use to calculate and then offer economically sound discounts to both new and repeat customers 'on the spot' and without the need for approval delays. I don't know if it would take the form of an app for the sales reps' phones or some type of worksheet, but the ability to close the deal quickly should give us a leg up."

"No doubt." Alex thought for a few moments. "We do have an awful lot of those small customers, and this doesn't seem like the kind of offer you could simply e-mail or snail mail to them. It's somewhat complicated—at least a lot different than what they'd be familiar with. Someone would have to explain it and, perhaps, it's rationale to the customers."

"You've got a point there," replied Marcella. "I hadn't thought of that. Kelsey might have, but we didn't discuss it at all."

"I'll stop by and talk to her about this discounting scheme. I like it. I have an idea that might work."

"Are you going to save it for her, or give me a preview?"

"I'll bounce it off of you first and see what you think."

"Okay, shoot!"

Alex began, "The customers we're targeting are most likely phoning in orders that are taken by our four customer service reps. Now it's the phone-in orders that we're trying to minimize. As I recall, they're the most expensive orders to process. So a lot of our target customers are contacting us—we won't need to reach out to them if we can trigger the process at the point that they are phoning in an order."

"So we'd need to get the customer service reps up to speed and create a process that would enable us to quickly react when a customer wants to take advantage of our offer."

"Not just up to speed," said Alex, "but incentivized. I'm sure they're all solid, loyal employees and have the company's best interests in mind, but this would be extra work for them, and human nature causes people to balk at extra work when there's no real incentive for them to do it."

"Do you have anything in mind?" asked Marcella.

"Oh, nothing specific, but I think something simple could be set up. Say a $20 or $25 bonus for each customer-order type and/or order-frequency change initiated by the rep. There'd need to be a delay—maybe three to six months—between the customer agreeing to the change and the bonus payment so we can make sure the customer actually does change. That could be an issue. Anyway, it's just an idea. I'll talk with Kelsey about it and see if she's got either a better idea or some ways to patch up the shortcomings in mine."

"Sounds like a good plan."

"And I like the idea of the sales reps having some type of tool to make on-the-spot discounting offers," added Alex. "I suppose you and Jim will work with Kelsey on that?"

"That's the idea," answered Marcella.

"Great! How about your conversation with Rich? Did the model's results give him any ideas for improving distribution?"

"As a matter of fact, they did. You know, I think going through this process over the past 20 months or so has made Rich feel less of an ugly duckling. I got the sense that he felt the company viewed distribution as a stepchild, a second-class citizen compared to manufacturing. He was there at staff meetings, but he didn't really participate much. I don't ever remember him proposing any ideas or requesting any capital to improve things in the warehouse. He was just there and answered questions when asked. But now you can't shut him up!"

They both laughed.

"I noticed the change in him, too," said Alex. "He's always quite anxious to report what's going on in the warehouse, feels comfortable enough to ask some pretty insightful questions of the others, and generally acts as if he's part of the team, not just an observer."

"You know," said Marcella, "I believe this is the only place Rich has ever worked, and until you arrived, he'd only experienced Jake's rather authoritarian style of management. It was 'show up, don't think, and just do what I tell you to do.' No one really asked him his opinion or encouraged him to come up with ideas on his own. I'm not sure he knew how to handle the culture change."

"Don't discount your part in this," replied Alex. "You've treated him as an equal partner in the development of the new cost model. You've shown respect for his knowledge and experience. You've incorporated his ideas into the model and sought his ideas for improving the warehouse's operation. And I believe having his own measurements has given him the feeling that he's actually an executive managing distribution, not just someone babysitting the warehouse. You've pushed the right buttons."

"I don't know about that," replied Marcella, somewhat embarrassed.

"I do," responded Alex. "Now how about Rich's ideas for improvement?"

She then proceeded to detail Rich's thoughts about reducing the handling required between a product's being packaged in manufacturing and tucked away in its cube; his plan to find ways to streamline order picking, perhaps with the aid of some new capital; and his plan to subdivide cubes so that slow-moving items would require less warehouse space.

"Those all sound like worthwhile endeavors. I don't think he would have thought of them without the information from your new model."

"*Our* new model!" snapped Marcella. "It's *our* model, not mine."

"Okay, our model then. He must be working with Chris on some of those. I've seen them huddled together a lot lately."

"Oh, I'm sure of that. I think he always viewed Chris as a competitor before. Now he views him as an ally. Especially after I mentioned that it was Chris' opinion that Rich had been shortchanged on capital spending all these years."

"Chris said that?"

"I didn't make it up."

"Did you ever hear of Bo Schembechler?"

"Bo Schembechler? Can't say that I have. Who is he?"

"He was the University of Michigan's football coach back in the '70s and '80s."

"What about him?"

"I had an officer who served under me in the Navy who had played for Bo. He liked to quote from a speech Bo once gave to his players. He said, 'No man is more important than the team. No coach is more important than the team. It's the team! The team! The team!' Well, I think you and your peers are fast becoming a team. I really like that."

"Weren't we a team before?"

"That's not what I saw when I arrived. You were a group of capable individuals all trying to do a good job while working in your silos. Your efforts were disconnected from each other.

Now, due to a great extent to the work you've done in getting everyone involved in this cost model, I can see a real team evolving. You're beginning to work as a coordinated unit for the good of the whole. I see that as a major step in ensuring the long-term success of PlumbCo."

Marcella wasn't sure how to respond.

"Now," continued Alex, "what ideas has Chris come up with after seeing what the model has to say?"

"He's concerned with the 20% indirect activity allowance. He and Jim used the model to figure out that we could save $170,000 if we could reduce it to 10%. So he's going to dig into it, beginning with the development of a new efficiency report that breaks out capacity utilization, equipment efficiency, and labor efficiency by manufacturing activity."

"Wow, $170,000! That's a lot of money."

"It's a reduction of about 2 people and a 4% reduction in overtime. We might not realize the savings immediately, but as we grow, we can produce more products without increasing the labor force.

"He also thinks we can get rid of two of our mid-sized presses, generate some cash, and still have plenty of open capacity to accommodate growth."

"Someone in manufacturing voluntarily offering to get rid of equipment? That's a first. I've always found that manufacturing people like to hoard equipment. They never want to get rid of anything."

Marcella laughed. "I don't think Chris is your ordinary manufacturing guy."

"I believe you've got him pegged," replied Alex. "Any other ideas?"

"He had one more," replied Marcella, "but I promised I wouldn't mention it to anyone."

"Did it have something to do with outsourcing some of our slow-moving products?"

"As a matter of fact, it did."

"He asked me what I thought of the idea."

"What was your answer?"

"I told him it was worth looking into, but I'd be pretty careful about it. I'm not real comfortable with the risks involved. You've got to be damn sure the supplier can meet our quality standards and our schedules. But if the numbers say it's a good move and the risks are minimal, I might go along with the idea."

Alex hesitated for a moment and then said, "I've got one more question for you. And this is in confidence. Just between you and me."

"Okay, shoot," replied Marcella.

"You know I'll be sitting in this chair only for another year or so. Jake and I want to find someone we believe can fill the role of CEO at PlumbCo for at least the next decade. You've gotten to know all the players here inside the company. Is there anyone you believe we should consider?"

Marcella was a bit startled and surprised that Alex would ask her such a question. Why would they seek her opinion? She was just the controller. What did she know about the qualities needed in a CEO? But he did ask, so after a bit of thought, she answered.

"I don't really know what you believe makes for a good CEO, but I think Chris Scheele would be the guy. He's good to work with. He thinks outside the box. Sometimes, I think he understands financial concepts better than I do. As far as I can tell, everyone respects him. From our discussions, I know he understands how what he does impacts the rest of the organization and takes that into account. He also give serious consideration to 'the numbers' when making decisions and doesn't just rely on experience and intuition. Yes, I think Chris would be the prime in-house candidate."

"I appreciate your input," said Alex. "We're in the early stages right now, but from a strategic standpoint, it's the number one issue on the Board's priority list, and the more input we can get, the better. You've been around here for about five years now and have gotten to know everyone pretty well. You've got a feel for their strengths and weaknesses. We all agreed that your input would be important."

"Anything else?" asked Marcella.

"Nope. It sounds like our new cost model has generated a lot of ideas and momentum. It'll be interesting to see how the actions it generates will impact the organization over the next year or so."

Chapter 45

It was the week before Thanksgiving and the last IMA Chapter meeting before the holiday break. Chapter members had all been duly briefed on the changes in both state and federal tax laws, and they were milling around in small groups, passing along holiday greetings and carrying on private discussions before heading home. As she had done for nearly two years now, Marcella was keeping her eye out for the Major. She very much wanted him to know about all of the actions being taken as a result of the information generated by their new cost model. As the crowd thinned out, she took a quick look into the lounge and saw him there in his usual spot, sipping on a Manhattan, with a glass of Chardonnay waiting for her.

"Delighted to see you again, Mrs. DeCou." The Major stood up as she arrived. "And how were the speakers this evening?"

"Well, you don't exactly expect captivating speakers when the subject is taxes," she laughed, "but they weren't too bad. How've you been?"

"Oh, busy as usual," he replied. She only wished she knew what this mysterious old gent was busy at. The way he had been able to avoid answering questions as to his business or personal background made it pretty clear he had no intention of revealing much about himself, and she certainly didn't want to jeopardize her friendship with him by prying too much.

"I would imagine," he continued, "that you've been able to discuss the results of your modeling efforts with your peers and determine whether it has provided them with any actionable insights."

"That's for sure. I've been looking forward to telling you about it. At this point in the process, I'm not surprised at how well everything has been received, but it has turned out a lot better than I would have imagined when we started 20 or so months ago. The team has really bought in."

"I believe that might be a testament to the way you've gone about it," replied the Major. "You haven't created a model on your own and then imposed it on them; you've developed the model with them and adopted it as a team. It's theirs as much as it is yours. In the process, you've made them believe. They believe that the numbers are correct. That they represent economic reality. That they are important to consider when evaluating possible actions or making decisions. You've created an environment in which managerial costing information can be put to its best use."

"I don't know about that," she blushed a bit. "I was just doing my job."

"Ah, but that's it. So many people in your position don't see it as their job. They process the transactions, close the books, do the taxes, prepare the standard financial statements, file the other required reports, and do all the things necessary to keep the company in compliance with rules and regulations. They help measure and protect value, but they do nothing to *create* value. That's all their management expects of them, so that's all they do. Did you ever hear of 'The Pygmalion Effect'?"

"No. Does it have something to do with Eliza Doolittle and Henry Higgins?"

The Major chuckled, "No. It's basically the observation that expectations influence performance. It's named after the Greek myth of Pygmalion, a sculptor who creates an ivory statue representing his ideal of womanhood and then falls in love with his own creation. He firmly believes the statue can be brought to life and, eventually, the goddess Venus brings it to life for him. The myth is an allegory for the very accurate observation that higher expectations lead to achievement and low expectations undermine achievement.

"As it applies to your situation," he continued, "your boss, Alex, let you know in a very subtle way that his expectations for PlumbCo's controller were a lot more than just being a glorified bookkeeper. He wanted his controller to be a value-adding member of management. Had he not done so, I expect you'd still be limiting yourself to the controller's traditional role and performing as a very competent measurer and protector of value. Instead, you rose to meet his expectations."

"You're right," said Marcella, "it took a nudge from Alex to head me in the right direction, but once I embarked on the trip, it turned out to be a lot more interesting and rewarding than sitting in my office and counting the beans."

"And," the Major added, "I hope your trip continues. That it's just the first leg on a long voyage you'll be on for several decades. But tell me about the results of your model."

Marcella told the Major about her meetings with Kelsey, Rich, Chris, and Alex, and the actions that were either being taken or considered as a result of the model's insights. When she was finished, she looked up and saw a broad grin on the Major's face.

"Well done, Grasshopper!" he said.

"Well done, what?"

"I said, 'Well done, Grasshopper.' I apologize. That phrase was probably popular way before your time. I keep forgetting how many more years I've been around than you. Look it up online." He paused for a moment. "You know, Mrs. DeCou, I'm going to miss you."

"Miss me?" Marcella exclaimed with surprise. "What do you mean, 'you're going to miss me'?"

"I'm afraid you've done so well that my tenure as your mentor has come to an end. It's time for me to move on to others who require my help."

"So you won't be coming to the IMA chapter meetings anymore?"

"I'm afraid I've never been at one of your chapter meetings."

"But I've seen you there."

"You may have seen me, but I wasn't there."

"I'm confused. It sounds like you're talking nonsense."

"Oh, I'm aware that it sounds like nonsense, but it is true." The Major hesitated for a few moments, took a sip of his Manhattan, and said, "I guess there's no harm in telling you this. You see, I was sent here because you needed some help and began asking questions of your fellow IMA chapter members. Your fervent desire to learn more was detected, and I was sent here to help you along."

"Sent? By whom?"

"That's not important. The fact is that you sincerely wanted help, and I was available to provide that help. You see, I became passionate about the measurement and use of cost information long before you were born. I spent the bulk of my professional life promoting the development and use of logically derived cost information. I even founded an organization dedicated to spreading the science of cost accounting. That's what I called it back then, 'the science of cost accounting.' Unfortunately, I didn't get to see it grow and flourish. I passed through to the other side shortly thereafter."

"You passed through to the other side?" asked Marcella. "What do you mean?"

The Major smiled. "I guess you'd say I died. But the folks on that side of the veil want the souls there to be happy, and they realized that I had been happiest when I was making others aware of the benefits of cost accounting and teaching them how to incorporate its principles into the management of their organizations. So they've allowed me to continue doing it all these years."

Marcella had become more curious than shocked.

"How many years has that been?" she asked.

"It's been nearly a century now. I've had a chance to mentor many of the people you read about in the development of managerial costing—that's what they like to call it today."

Marcella still wasn't certain whether or not he was pulling her leg.

"Did they give you credit for helping them? I've never heard mention of anyone called 'the Major' being involved in the development of costing concepts."

"None of them remember their conversations we had together."

"That's pretty ungrateful."

"No," he replied, "they're not being ungrateful. They literally don't remember the time we spent together. They remember the results of our conversations, but not that we had them. I'm afraid it will be the same with you. You won't remember me at all. I will simply fade from your memory."

Marcella was getting a bit concerned. She thought, *Maybe the old gentleman was starting to go a bit gaga?*

"But I've mentioned you to many of the other people I've worked with as well as others here at the chapter meetings."

"They won't remember either," replied the Major. "That's the way it works. We get to mentor others with a sincere passion for our former areas of expertise and keep that area growing. That's our reward."

"You said 'we.' There are others?"

"Oh, many others." The Major laughed. "I'm sure you've heard the expression 'standing on the shoulders of giants.' Well, I don't consider myself to be a 'giant,' but that expression is more literally true than you might think. It happens in all walks of life. Fortunately, in my case, the organization I founded provides those shoulders for many in your profession. I only come and visit those deemed to be special: individuals like you."

Marcella look down at her drink for a moment, considering the things the Major had said. Her thoughts were interrupted suddenly by a voice.

"Don't you think it's time we packed up and headed home?" It was her friend Caroline Perry. "We've both got to get up for work tomorrow."

Marcella was vaguely surprised to see Caroline, but she wasn't sure why. "Oh, yeah. It is getting late, isn't it?"

"I guess we won't be able to get together again until after the holidays."

"Probably not. I hope you and your family have a great Thanksgiving and Christmas season."

"Same to you," replied Caroline. "We've got family coming in from out of town, so I hope the weather won't be too bad. A little snow for a white Christmas, but hopefully nothing more."

"I'll sign up for that," replied Marcella.

Marcella still felt a little uneasy as the two friends headed for their cars, but by the time she got home, that uneasy feeling had faded away.

Chapter 46

The next 15 months were a period of significant change at PlumbCo as the actions prompted by insights gleaned from the new cost model were carried out. Pricing practices were adjusted, operating improvements initiated, unneeded equipment sold, parts outsourced, and changes made in material handling. The books had just been closed for the year, and Alex decided it was a good time to meet with his management group to review the year's results. He also wanted to get a feel for how the new cost model had affected the way each staff member viewed the business and the level of confidence they had in the model moving forward.

"Man, is it cold out!" said Alex as the members of his staff assembled in the conference room. "The only good part of February is the last week."

"Why the last week?" asked Rich Vivian.

"Because that's when I go to Arizona to try and get my golf game in shape for the coming year."

"Does it work?" enquired Kelsey Hayes.

"Not usually," laughed Alex, "but I use it as an excuse for getting somewhere warmer about this time of year. I'd stay longer, but I've got to be back here for the annual meeting in March."

The group was assembled. It included Marcella, Rich Vivian, Kelsey Hayes, and Chris Scheele. Jim Stinson was also invited to participate, in case anyone needed some help in accessing or "crunching" numbers.

"Marcella, how about a quick summary of the year's results?"

Marcella passed out a one-page summary comparing the year's results with the results of the previous year.

"As you can see," she began, "our sales were up $2 million, or 10%, from the previous year while our profit before taxes and interest increased by about 35%. Profit as a percentage of sales increased from 10.6% to 13.1%, but I believe more important, our profit as a percentage of value added increased from 22.2% to 29.9%."

"Why do you say the profit as a percentage of value added is more important?" asked Kelsey.

"Because it's a better indicator of how well we're using our investment. It's not perfect, but it does track return on investment much better than the old 'percent-of-sales' calculation."

"Why is that?" Kelsey responded.

Alex didn't want the meeting to veer too far off the course he intended it to take, so he thought it best to get it back on track quickly.

"Marcella has explained the rationale to me, and I agree with her. At this point, let's just assume she's correct and move on. We can have her explain the important difference between the two measures at our next staff meeting." He looked at Marcella. "Carry on," he said.

"It's interesting that we were able to increase our sales volume by 10% with no additional manufacturing equipment and no additional production labor. Our only headcount increase was the addition of one warehouse worker mid-year. I think it's important to recognize that $1 million of our $22 million in sales was from selling products that we did not manufacture in-house. That's a big change from the past when we manufactured all of the products we sold. That means our manufacturing volume was only 5% higher despite the 10% increase in sales. I also find it pretty impressive that the 5% increase in production required only about $45,000 in additional operation costs—a slight increase in overtime worked by existing production personnel and an additional $30,000 or so in utilities and supplies."

"Chris," it was Alex jumping in, "how was it possible to increase production by 5% with such a small increase in cost?"

"I believe much of it was due to the work we did to eat away at the indirect activity allowance," he replied. "That 20% number stuck in my craw. I realize that there will always be more labor required than is theoretically necessary, but the 20% seemed awfully excessive to me."

"So you've been able to reduce it?" asked Alex.

"We've made a dent in it," replied Chris. He looked at Jim. "What's it down to now, Jim?"

"It's down to about 15% for the year," answered Jim, "but it's been down in the 12% area in recent months."

"What did you do to get it down so far?" asked Alex.

"Jim and I came up with some new measures for efficiency. We did it by equipment category, and we also separated it into equipment efficiency and labor efficiency. Those new measures did several things for us. For one, I can now zero in on areas where the difference between theoretical and actual labor is the greatest. It's no longer just one plant-wide measure. That alone helped me identify the areas where production labor was often idled while equipment was setting up or down for some other reason and where actual crew sizes were higher than those required by the process. We're now providing the area supervisors with daily statistics showing how effectively the workers assigned to them are performing. They're now paying close attention to something they paid little or no attention to before.

"It's also given me a better handle on the difference between the number of hours a piece of equipment is dedicated to a particular job and the hours it is actually running that job. Getting some of those issues under control has enabled us to come up with firmer production schedules that enable us to have less 'cushion' in the number of production workers that need to be on-site each day."

"How low do you think you can get the percentage?" asked Alex.

"I'm shooting for 10%. Once we get it there, I think the solutions will be much tougher. I don't necessarily consider what we've done so far to be 'low-hanging fruit,' but we haven't spent any money to make any of the changes. We've just begun measuring things differently and paying attention to more details than before. Once we get to 10%, we'll still look for improvements, but we will be getting closer to whatever the inherent minimum level of indirect activity allowance is for molding."

"Ten percent sounds pretty good to me," replied Alex. "How has our new sub-contractor for slow-moving parts worked out?"

"I was a bit nervous about that move," replied Chris. "It made sense 'by the numbers,' but I was a bit hesitant because of the risk involved. Fortunately, we were able to locate a very reputable and financially stable rubber molder that's been in business for over 30 years that was willing to work with us, providing we could guarantee a minimum volume of work. We outsourced 375 of our SKUs to them and guaranteed to buy at least 60,000 total units from them annually. We then devised a monthly order-point, order-quantity system with them. These parts move slowly enough that restocking doesn't need to be done any more often than that. So far, it's worked out great. Although I'll always be somewhat nervous when everything isn't taking place under our roof, I'm much more comfortable than I thought I'd be."

"That's good to hear. And you're still confident that selling those two mid-sized presses was the right thing to do?"

"As confident as I was at the time I sold them last spring. We've got enough capacity left with the three presses we still have to handle about 30% more business than we currently have without working any overtime. I think that'll take care of us for some time."

"That's good, especially since the $60,000 raised by selling them helped fund the improvements we made in moving product from the manufacturing floor to the warehouse. Want to elaborate on that?"

"I think I'll let Rich talk about that. He's the guy who came up with the idea, which, I believe, has worked out very well."

"Rich," said Alex, "what say you?"

Rich hesitated a bit as he began to speak. He was still getting used to being considered a key member of management and being asked for his input.

"Well," he started, "it seemed that there was an awful lot of unnecessary handling and sorting going on between Chris' workers and mine. A lot of 'pick 'em up and put 'em downs' as well as staging and re-staging of pallets. My thought was that it would be much more efficient if manufacturing just sent the products to us immediately after production and we picked it up from there. I believe there were usually three moves required to get product from the floor to the warehouse, and to me, that seemed like two moves too many.

"Chris and I had quite a few conversations about what we could do to eliminate the two extra moves when one of us, I don't remember who, came up with the idea of having gravity-roller conveyors linking the plant floor and the warehouse."

"It was your idea, Rich," interjected Chris. "I just agreed it was a good one."

"Okay, I guess it was my idea." Rich smiled at Chris. He was pretty generous at passing the credit around. "So we purchased and installed a system of gravity rollers so that production could move product directly from the packaging cells to the rollers. Gravity then delivers the product to the warehouse, where we sort it and deliver it to its cube. I believe the one move still made by manufacturing takes longer than the earlier moves, so we're not reducing the handling in the plant by two-thirds, but I bet it's a good 55%-65% less than before."

"I'll agree with that." It was Chris again, adding his confirmation to Rich's estimate.

"Does it add to the amount of work you have to do in the warehouse?" asked Alex.

"None at all. The amount of time we spend in receiving and putting away the products is just about the same as it was before."

"Good," said Alex. "Didn't you do something to save storage space as well?"

"That we did. We increased our storage capacity by 225 cubes by subdividing 75 cubes into quarters and placing 300 of our small, slow-moving products into those quarter-cubes.

I don't believe the move saves us any money right now, but it does make better use of storage space, and it will reduce storage costs in the future."

"Kelsey," Alex looked toward his director of sales, "sales are up but profits are up more. What's your take on that?"

"Obviously, the actions taken by Chris and Rich have a lot to do with it, but I think the changes we made in our discounting practices helped a lot as well."

"Remind us what those changes were."

"Sure. Our first initiative was to turn as many of our money-losing or marginally profitable small customers into money makers as possible. The customer profitability analyses Jim was able to develop for each customer highlighted those that needed to be addressed and the reasons they were a problem. I was a bit intimidated at first because each customer's case was unique and there were somewhere around 400 customers that we'd need to deal with one on one. Fortunately, Marcella and Alex made suggestions that turned my impossible task into one that was easily executed. Marcella pointed out that the major problem was with small customers who ordered frequently by mail or over the telephone. If we could get the majority of them to order once every quarter electronically, we could reduce the cost of serving that group significantly.

"To induce them to change, we'd need to offer them a discount that made the change worth their while. Jim helped me work out a flat discount we could offer that would enable us to keep an average of about 60% of the overall savings. It was possible that having some customers accept the discount might reduce their profitability, but making the same offer to all target accounts would save a lot of time and effort, and we believed the increased profitability of the others would more than offset the negative impact of those few customers."

Alex smiled and asked, "How'd you go about contacting all those customers and inducing them to modify their ordering practices?"

"That's where your idea came into play," she replied. "Marcella passed on your suggestion that we bring our customer service reps up to speed on the plan; provide them with the tools needed to process any agreed-to discounts on the spot; have them mention the availability of the added discount if orders were submitted electronically once per quarter when one of the target customers phones in their next order; and provide the rep with a bonus for each customer they get to change."

"And did my brilliant plan work?"

"Well, a handful of customers turned down the offer, but the vast majority signed on. And all but a few did, indeed, change their ordering practices. The customer profitability profiles for the customers that did change improved considerably for all but a few of the accounts. And the additional cost to us was about $10,000 in bonuses for the reps."

"May I add something here, Kelsey?" It was Jim Stinson speaking.

"Sure, Jim," she answered.

Jim began, "The customer cost profiles show us that almost all of those customers accepting our proposal have gone from being poor or marginal customers to valuable customers in our portfolio of business. However, it doesn't indicate whether or not we're actually making more money as a result of the changes. There are a few statistics that might give us a better feel for how the change has impacted the company overall."

"And they are?" asked Alex.

"There are three interesting statistics. First, our sales were up by 10%, but the number of orders we processed was down by 4%. So the sales per order increased considerably. That's one positive statistic. Second, the number of electronic orders went up by 15% while the number of non-electronic orders decreased by 33%. So not only was the cost of each order spread over more units, the cost of the average order dropped considerably. Finally, our 10% increase in sales resulted in only 5% more line items being picked. So the average units per line item rose as well. Put them all together, and we've decreased the cost of serving these customers considerably."

"One thing to keep in mind," interjected Marcella, "is that this might not show as a reduction in cost on our financials. After all, we still have the same number of people in customer service taking orders, and we actually added someone in the warehouse in the middle of the year. What it does tell us is that we will be able to handle a much higher volume of sales with little or no increase in customer service cost. We'll make better use of the resources we have."

"Good point," said Alex. "The improvements you've made all won't necessarily impact the bottom line immediately, but they will have an impact as we move forward." He looked toward Kelsey. "How about our larger customers? Any luck with them?"

"We can't offer them the same 'one-size-fits-all' discount that we offer the smaller customers. We have to craft a specific plan for each one as our existing agreements with them come up for renewal. So the process has been slower. In addition, many of them are already significant value-adding customers in our portfolio, so we don't even bring up the topic with them.

However, we are slowly getting some of the marginal ones to change. I believe 90% to 95% of the improvements Jim talked about are due to the changes we've made with that group of smaller accounts. They're the ones whose order processing and fulfillment costs were eating away at our profits."

Alex leaned back in his chair and stared at the ceiling for a few seconds. He then slowly and deliberately looked in turn at each individual in the room before slamming both of his palms on the table and declaring, "You guys have done one helluva job! If this were the Navy, I'd give you all a medal."

Everyone laughed.

"No, really," he continued, "in the three years I've been here, you've all grown tremendously as individuals and as a team. I was pretty confident when I arrived that you all were good at what you did; I'm sure Jake made sure of that. But your jobs were pretty much to do as you were told. You weren't asked for your opinions. You weren't asked for your ideas. You weren't asked to make any significant decisions. You weren't asked to work in concert with other parts of the organization. Just show up, shut up, and do your job.

"Now I look around this table, and I see a team of highly competent individuals who can work together as a unit; who can work out solutions to attain organizational goals; who can make important decisions in concert with their peers; who understand how to incorporate data and analytics into their decision-making processes. I see a team capable of leading this organization into a highly successful future."

He paused for about thirty seconds and looked at each person at the table once again.

"That's it," he said abruptly. "That's all the accolades for now. Your job now is to not let up. Keep getting better. Keep making PlumbCo better. You won't be able to do it on your own. You'll need each other. There's a lot more potential than one might think in this sleepy little rubber molder. Now get back to work." He smiled. "I've got to start packing for Arizona."

As the team filed out of the conference room, Alex gave each member a big hug.

Chapter 47

Each March, it was Marcella's job to present the company's financial results for the previous year to PlumbCo's Board of Directors. It wasn't really a big deal. Everyone there would have already seen the results and had their questions about those results answered. And it wasn't actually a formal Board of Directors. It was more like an informal get-together of Jake Ullrey and his wife Catherine, Alex, someone from PlumbCo's bank, and a couple of Jake's business friends. As the normal routine went, she was first on the agenda, presented the results, answered a few easy questions, and then headed back to her office. She had no idea what they talked about afterward.

This time, however, it was different. Even though the meeting was set to start at two o'clock, her instructions were to come to the conference room at four o'clock. She was curious about the change in schedule. Could it be that something really important would be discussed? Might Jake be planning on selling the business? Or was a new investor getting involved? Maybe they were going to interview candidates for replacing Alex. After all, he wasn't planning on sitting in the CEO's chair for much longer.

Four o'clock arrived and she made her way to the conference room. She knocked and the door was opened by a tall, dark man she didn't recognize.

"Mrs. DeCou, I presume?" he asked while sporting a wide grin.

"Yes," she replied.

"Please come in. I believe you're expected."

She entered the room and saw Alex.

"Marcella," he said. "You're here. I see you've met Theron."

"We haven't exactly been introduced," replied the doorkeeper, "as far as she knows, I'm your new butler."

Alex laughed. "Oh. In that case, Marcella, meet Theron Papasifakis. Theron, meet Marcella DeCou."

"I can't tell you how glad I am to finally meet you," said Theron as he shook Marcella's hand. "You've been the topic of conversation over drinks on the 19th hole at the club for a couple of years now."

"I have?" replied Marcella, much surprised.

"Oh, yes. Being well aware of what I think about accountants, Alex has been keeping me apprised at how you've been shattering my long-held, rather negative image of people in your profession. I believe he takes delight in trying to prove me wrong."

"Oh, don't pay any attention to him," said Alex. "He's just being silly." He turned to look at Theron and asked, "You Greeks can be silly, can't you? That title's not restricted to Englishmen."

Marcella was beginning to wonder if they had spent the first two hours of the meeting as if they were on that 19th hole. But just then, the door opened and her former boss, Jake Ullrey, entered.

"Marcella! It's good to see you again. It must be six months since I saw you."

"Just about six months. I think it was the company picnic back in August."

"I believe you're right. Everything good with you and the family?"

"Paul and the kids are doing great, and I'm not going to complain," she replied.

"Now that you're back, Jake," interrupted Alex, "we should probably move on to the reason we're here."

"That's probably not a bad idea. Marcella and I can catch up later."

"Is it just the three of you?" she asked as she began preparing to do her annual financial presentation. "Catherine isn't here? Or our bankers?"

"No," replied Alex, "it's just the three of us. And don't bother with your presentation. Just have a seat. We've got other things to discuss."

No presentation? thought Marcella. *Other things to discuss? Maybe Jake has sold the company. But what's Alex's buddy Papasifakis doing here? He's not on the Board.* Her mind was running a mile a minute as she sat down.

"To start," said Alex, "I'm going to talk a little bit about you and your work since I've been here at PlumbCo."

Uh-oh, she thought, *did I screw something up?*

"It was pretty obvious after I'd been here a few months that Jake had assembled a cadre of very capable individuals to head up the various functions in the company, but he had never really attempted to mold them into a cohesive, goal-focused management team. He and I talked about the situation, and he acknowledged that his leadership style was pretty autocratic. He hadn't really given much thought to developing an organization that could operate effectively without his day-to-day involvement. We both agreed that we needed to correct that situation, so my major goal over the past few years was to try and mold the company into an organization that could continue to be successful on its own."

Marcella looked at Jake, who smiled and nodded to indicate his agreement with Alex.

Alex continued, "One of the key parts of my task was to determine whether or not there was someone within the company who could lead it into the future. Someone who had the respect of the company's other key executives. Someone who showed the ability to lead a talented group of technicians and managers and have them operate as a team. Someone who respected the ability and opinions of the people he or she would lead and could balance them effectively in arriving at a decision. Someone who understood how all the parts of an organization fit together to optimize the performance of the whole. Someone the other leaders in the company would follow. If we couldn't identify one, we'd need to look outside for someone we believe could do the job.

"I also convinced Jake that he needed to put together a real Board of Directors to support whoever becomes the new CEO. A group of experienced executives who could provide input and advice when necessary, but who would not meddle in the day-to-day operations of the business. Individuals who would be on call if the CEO needed them, but would otherwise restrict themselves to policy-level issues."

"Alex's leadership experience really opened my eyes," interjected Jake. "My objective was to personally control everything.

Unfortunately, that type of leadership doesn't lead to developing new leaders. I was lucky Alex was willing to act as CEO for a few years. I think I've learned more about managing during his time as CEO than I did all the time I was actually running things."

"So," said Alex, "the first thing we did when we met today was elect a new Board of Directors. Theron agreed to join Jake and me as its members. We decided to limit the Board to the three of us for the time being." Alex looked at Jake and smiled, "At least for today.

"Jake provides the Board with his years of experience, his understanding of the issues faced by PlumbCo, and his institutional memory. Theron provides us with his wealth of management experience and his outsider's point of view. I'm not sure what I provide," Alex laughed. "I was just another guy in the room when they were looking for a third person."

"Our first decision as a Board," said Jake, "was to decide what we would do about a new CEO to replace Alex when he steps down next month."

Marcella quickly turned to Alex, "You're stepping down that soon?" She had no idea his departure date was that imminent.

"That soon," answered Alex. "The golf season gets going around here in April, and when the weather breaks, I want to be on the golf course and not in the corner office."

"He wants to lose money instead of make money," interjected Theron.

"We'll see about that," laughed Alex.

Jake spoke again.

"We came to a decision. Marcella, we'd like you to become PlumbCo's new CEO."

Marcella was stunned.

"Me?" she asked. She had no idea this was coming. She assumed that if anyone would be promoted to the CEO position from within, it would be Chris Scheele.

"Yes, you," answered Jake. "And to be honest with you, you made the decision pretty easy. Over the past three years, we've seen you transform yourself from an accountant straight out of central casting into the company's most effective leader."

"You've changed your focus from counting beans to growing beans," added Theron.

"You may not fully realize how much you've grown in three years," said Alex. "Or maybe you haven't really grown that much. It may just be that you had the opportunity to put the leadership ability you've always had on display, and it showed. Let's itemize some of the key qualities we've seen in you that led us to our decision.

"In dealing with your peers, you've listened carefully to their issues and ideas and worked with them to address their concerns. You've partnered with them in addressing issues and developing solutions. You've let others get the credit for successes you've initiated, like during last month's annual review meeting. It was your model that was behind most of the improvements, but you didn't mention it at all. You've given people an opportunity to solve things on their own. And when they can't come up with a solution, you mentor them; you don't do it for them.

"As you've gotten closer to all the department heads, we've seen your focus evolve from purely financial to operational. You probably know more about each part of the organization than anyone but its functional head, and you do know more about how the parts work together to create an effective organization than anyone. You've been able to come up with practical solutions to problems. You haven't just looked for software to solve the problem or some current management fad to adopt.

"Your bailiwick is accounting, but you've managed to have a major influence over areas where you have no authority. All your peers trust both your character and your guidance."

Marcella had begun to blush. She heard what Alex was saying, but didn't think she had been doing anything special. She had simply been doing her job.

Alex continued, "Remember about a year ago when I asked you if you thought any current member of PlumbCo's management would make a good CEO?"

"Yeah. And I believe I said Chris Scheele would be a good choice."

"That's right. Over the past year, I've worked that question into conversations with every member of PlumbCo's management team. And everybody except you came up with the same answer. That answer was 'Marcella DeCou.' One of the most adamant was Chris. He said, 'Marcella is already the conductor who's leading this band. I don't see why she shouldn't be given the opportunity to do it officially.'"

"Chris said that?"

"You don't think I'd make up something like that, do you?"

"I don't know what to say," said Marcella. "This isn't something I was expecting or even thought possible."

"How about saying that you'll do it?" laughed Theron. "I'm finding it rather enjoyable having all my long-held, anti-accountant prejudices being annihilated."

"Yes, Marcella," said Jake. "We really think you're the right person for the job. We'll be available to support you when you ask, but we won't be looking over your shoulder and micromanaging. We'll be too busy golfing and, I hope, taking Alex's money when I win on the course."

"How can I say no?" she replied. "If you think I'm up to it, I'm game. Thank you for your confidence."

"Great," said Jake, "now let's celebrate. Paul should be waiting for us at the club."

"Paul? At the club? What's he doing at the club?"

"We took a chance that you'd accept the job," said Alex. "I called Paul this afternoon and gave him a heads-up so he could slip out of work early, get a sitter for your kids, and meet us at the club for a celebration. I told the receptionist at the club that he was my guest and to let him wait in the restaurant."

"You're all pretty sneaky, aren't you?" laughed Marcella.

They all got into Alex's car and headed to the club, where Paul greeted them as they entered the restaurant. The receptionist followed Alex into the restaurant and pulled him aside.

"Is the lady with you Mrs. DeCou?" she asked.

"Yes, why?" replied Alex.

"An older gentleman dropped off a package for her. He said she'd be arriving later today with you."

"An older gentleman? Who was it?"

"I didn't get a name. He wasn't a member. Just a very polite older man who dropped off the package, said she'd be coming with you later on today, and that this was a congratulatory gift for her."

Alex looked stupefied.

"Who in the world would know that we were coming and that congratulations would be in order? Did any of you spill the beans?"

Each of the men looked at each other and shrugged their shoulders.

"I don't think it could have been any of us," said Theron. "The three of us were together all afternoon, and Paul just found out what was going on a couple of hours ago."

The receptionist handed Marcella the box that had been left with her at the front desk.

"Who could this be from?" she said out loud.

"There's only one way to find out," answered Paul.

She opened the package. It was a bottle of Chardonnay—the same label they served at the Kingsley Inn, after her monthly IMA meetings. There was a card enclosed.

"What does the card say?" asked Jake.

"It says, 'Congratulations, Mrs. DeCou! I had great expectations for you, and you met every one of them.'"

"Is it signed?"

"Yes ..." Marcella hesitated.

"Who is it?" The men had all asked the same question in unison.

"I'm not sure," she answered. "It's just signed 'the Major.' Nothing else."

"Who's the Major?" asked Theron.

"I have no idea," replied Marcella. "Do any of you know someone known as 'the Major'?"

The all looked at each other and shook their heads.

"Well," suggested Alex, "let's leave this mystery for another day. It's time to celebrate our new CEO."